COLUMBIA COLLEGE CHICAGO

C0-DKL-831

JAN 0 2 2008

A BRIEFE AND SHORT INSTRUCTION OF THE
ART OF MUSICKE
BY ELWAY BEVIN

Music Theory in Britain, 1500–1700: Critical Editions

SERIES EDITOR

Jessie Ann Owens, University of California, Davis, USA

This series represents the first systematic attempt to present the entire range of theoretical writing about music by English, Scottish, Welsh and Irish writers from 1500 to 1700 in modern critical editions. These editions, which use original spelling and follow currently accepted practices for the publication of early modern texts, aim to situate the work in the larger historical context and provide a view of musical practices.

Also published in this series:

Synopsis of Vocal Musick by A.B. Philo-Mus.
Edited by Rebecca Herissone

A Briefe Introduction to the Skill of Song by William Bathe
Edited by Kevin C. Karnes

A New Way of Making Fowre Parts in Counterpoint by Thomas Campion
and *Rules how to Compose* by Giovanni Coprario
Edited by Christopher R. Wilson

Columbia College Library
600 South Michigan
Chicago, Il 60805

A Briefe and Short Instruction of the Art of Musicke

By Elway Bevin

Edited and with an Introduction by

DENIS COLLINS

ASHGATE

© Denis Collins 2007

All rights reserved. No part of this publication may be reproduced, stored in a retrieval system or transmitted in any form or by any means, electronic, mechanical, photocopying, recording or otherwise without the prior permission of the publisher.

Denis Collins has asserted his moral right under the Copyright, Designs and Patents Act, 1988, to be identified as the editor of this work.

Published by
Ashgate Publishing Limited
Gower House
Croft Road
Aldershot
Hampshire GU11 3HR
England

Ashgate Publishing Company
Suite 420
101 Cherry Street
Burlington, VT 05401-4405
USA

Ashgate website: http://www.ashgate.com

British Library Cataloguing in Publication Data
Collins, Denis Brian
  A briefe and short instruction of the art of musicke by
  Elway Bevin. – (Music theory in Britain, 1500–1700:
  critical editions)
  1. Bevin, Elway, ca. 1554–1638. Briefe and short
  instruction of the art of musicke 2. Music theory – Early
  works to 1800 3. Canon (Musical form)
  I. Title II. Bevin, Elway, ca. 1554–1638. Briefe and short
  instruction of the art of musicke
  781'.092

Library of Congress Cataloging-in-Publication Data
Collins, Denis, 1965–
  A briefe and short instruction of the art of musicke by Elway Bevin / by Denis Collins.
      p. cm. – (Music theory in Britain, 1500–1700. Critical editions)
  Includes bibliographical references (p.   ) and index.
  ISBN-13: 978-0-7546-5053-9 (alk. paper)
  1. Canon (Musical form)–Early works to 1800 2. Music theory–Early works to 1800
  3. Music theory–England–History–17th century I. Bevin, Elway, ca. 1554–1638. Briefe
  and short instrvction of the art of mvsicke. II. Title.

  MT59.C75 2007
  781–dc22

                                                                                    2006032275

ISBN 978-0-7546-5053-9

Printed and bound in Great Britain by MPG Books Ltd, Bodmin, Cornwall

Contents

List of Figures

Note: All figures are used by permission of the British Library. Figures 1, 3 and 4 are also published with permission of ProQuest Information and Learning Company. Further reproduction is prohibited without permission.

Series Editor's Preface

The purpose of this series is to provide critical editions of music theory in Britain (primarily England, but Scotland, Ireland and Wales also) from 1500 to 1700. By 'theory' is meant all sorts of writing about music, from textbooks aimed at the beginner to treatises written for a more sophisticated audience. These foundational texts have immense value in revealing attitudes, ways of thinking and even vocabulary crucial for understanding and analysing music. They reveal beliefs about the power of music, its function in society and its role in education, and they furnish valuable information about performance practice and about the context of performance. They are a window into musical culture every bit as important as the music itself.

The editions in this series present the text in its original form. That is, they retain original spelling, capitalization and punctuation, as well as certain salient features of the type, for example, the choice of font. A textual commentary in each volume offers an explication of difficult or unfamiliar terminology as well as suggested corrections of printing errors; the introduction situates the work and its author in a larger historical context.

Jessie Ann Owens
Professor of Music
Dean of Humanities, Arts and Cultural Studies
University of California, Davis, USA

Acknowledgements

It is with pleasure that I acknowledge the assistance of many people in the preparation of this edition. The staff of the Architecture Music Library at the University of Queensland, especially Ivana Mimović and Ryan Weymouth, helped greatly in obtaining microfilm copies of the treatise and other items necessary for the project. The staff at the British Library dealt with my queries ably and courteously during my visit in January 2004. I wish to thank Kevin C. Karnes and Philip Bračanin for reading earlier versions of the typescript and for making many valuable suggestions. I am very grateful to Jessie Ann Owens for her kind assistance and expert guidance through the later stages of this work. I am thankful to Bonnie J. Blackburn for her assistance, especially in identifying a set of canons by Fernando de las Infantas, and to Peter Bergquist for answering my queries on Lasso sources. Throughout my work on Bevin I have benefited enormously from the assistance and encouragement of Branka Pavlović. A Faculty Fellowship at the Centre for Critical and Cultural Studies at the University of Queensland from February to June 2005 provided an opportunity for dedicated work on the project.

Denis Collins

PART I

Introduction:
Elway Bevin and Canon in England

Background to Bevin

Elway Bevin was born *ca.* 1554 and appears to have spent most of his life as an organist and Master of the Choristers at Bristol Cathedral.[1] His place of birth is unknown; claims that he was a pupil of Thomas Tallis cannot be documented and need to be treated with caution.[2] There is also no evidence for the claim that his most famous pupil was William Child.[3] A composer of modest accomplishment, Bevin's extant works include anthems, Evening Services, miscellaneous keyboard pieces, a three-part consort work entitled 'Browning' and two *In nomines*.[4] Other works are lost, including two books of music including canons from *ca.* 1626 listed in the records of the Bodleian Library.[5]

---

[1]   A summary of Bevin's life can be found in Joseph Graham Hooper, *The Life and Work of Elway Bevin* (Bristol, 1971). Several details are disputed by Robert Ford, particularly Bevin's date of birth, which Ford suggests as *ca.* 1567, and the authorship of several compositions attributed to Elway that Ford assigns to his son Edward. See Robert Ford, 'Bevins, Father and Son', *Music Review* 43 (1982), 104–8.

[2]   Hooper traces this claim in Anthony à Wood's *Fasti Oxonienses* and in the histories of Hawkins and Burney, with the latter stating that it is 'discoverable by his works'. See Hooper, *Bevin*, 1. John Hawkins, *A General History of the Science and Practice of Music*, ed. Charles Cudworth, 2 vols. (New York: Dover, 1963), 505. Charles Burney, *A General History of Music from the Earliest Ages to the Present Period*, ed. Frank Mercer, 2 vols. (London: G. T. Foulis, 1935), 263. It is possible, though by no means certain, that Burney and Hawkins may have drawn some information from the short biography of Bevin given in British Library Add. 31403, a collection of keyboard pieces by composers active in the late sixteenth and early seventeenth centuries.

[3]   Hooper, *Bevin*, 5, states that Bevin would have had daily contact with Child, who was a chorister in Bristol from about 1616 to about 1620. However, Ian Spink doubts that Child was ever a chorister at Bristol Cathedral; see Spink, 'Child, William', *Grove Music Online*, ed. L. Macy. <http://www.grovemusic.com>, accessed 6 August 2005. Both Hooper and Spink agree that Child was apprenticed to Thomas Prince, a lay clerk at the cathedral.

[4]   Sources for these works and their attributions to Elway, Edward or other composers are discussed by both Hooper and Ford, who are in disagreement with each other. Hooper retains his attributions in his entry for Bevin in *Grove Music Online*. Some of Elway Bevin's compositions have appeared in nineteenth- and twentieth-century editions, such as the anthem 'Lord, who shall dwell in thy Tabernacle', ed. Maurice Bevan, *Oxford Anthems* (London: Oxford University Press, 1963); 'Evening Service in the Dorian Mode', ed. C. F. Simkins et al., *Yearbook Press Series of Anthems and Church Music* (London: Ascherberg, Hopwood & Crew, 1963); 'A Canon, Four Parts to the Plain Song', in *Catches and Rounds by Old Composers Adapted to Modern Words*, ed. Thomas Oliphant (London: Calkin & Budd et al., 1840); 'Browning' can be found in *Musica Britannica*, 9: Jacobean Consort Music, ed. Thurston Dart and William Coates (London: Stainer and Bell, 1955; rev. 1962, 1971), 19–21.

[5]   Hooper, *Bevin*, 22. He cites Bodleian manuscript Mus. Sch. D.203.

Bevin's reputation rests primarily on his large output of canons. The extant canons are preserved in his 1631 treatise *A Briefe and Short Instruction of the Art of Musicke*, which is almost entirely dedicated to canonic writing over a plainsong, and in British Library RM 24.c.14, a collection of 300 short canons over plainsongs. Other manuscripts contain miscellaneous canons by Elway and his son Edward.[6]

A Briefe and Short Instruction was published when Bevin was an old man, possibly in his seventies. On the last page of this work he indicated that he wished to undertake a further publication of canons, but this never materialized. Bevin's last years appear to have been marred by problems associated with his supposed Catholicism. He was dismissed from his post as organist and choirmaster in 1637, and when he died the following year he was buried in a nearby parish church rather than in Bristol Cathedral. As Hooper remarks, 'Everything indicates yet nothing proves that Bevin was a life long recusant',[7] and it is impossible to determine the extent to which this might have influenced his career.

Bevin dedicated *A Briefe and Short Instruction* to Godfrey Goodman (1583–1656), who became bishop of Gloucester in 1624 and who was suspected of converting to the Roman Catholic faith.[8] Goodman may have assisted Bevin to become Gentleman Extraordinary of the Chapel Royal in 1605, an honorary position very likely reflecting the high esteem in which Bevin was held by his contemporaries.[9] Bevin states in the dedication that he has 'beene much bound for many favours' to Goodman, and it is possible that Goodman was among those who 'perswaded me to expose it [*i.e.*, the treatise] to the world'. In the address to the reader, Bevin's confidence in the merits of his work is reflected in the comment 'for though it be but small in quantity, yet for diversities of examples and difficulties, the quality may seeme the greater, and passe the elaborate workes of larger volumes'.

Bevin's treatise is one of about a dozen late sixteenth- and early seventeenth-century English music instruction books that present advanced material rather than merely the rudiments aimed at beginners. No modern edition of *A Briefe and Short Instruction* exists. Bevin's focus on canon was quite narrow compared with the broader range of topics covered by contemporary theorists. His work

---

   [6]   British Library Add. 31403 contains a 'Dubble canon or 4 p[ar]tes in two' on fol. 21[r] by Elway. A two-part canon at the fifth above on *Miserere*, fol. 12[r], and a two-part unison canon on fols. 18[v]–19[r] are by Edward. Other miscellaneous canons by Elway include a 20-part example in British Library Add. 29996, fol. 136[r], and a three-part canon in York Minster Library M.31(s). Facsimiles of both of these are in Hooper, *Bevin*, plates 11 and 8 respectively.

   [7]   Hooper, *Bevin*, 5.

   [8]   It is not clear whether Goodman fully embraced Roman Catholicism or merely maintained a flirtation with it. See Geoffrey Ingle Soden, *Godfrey Goodman: Bishop of Gloucester, 1583–1656* (London: S.P.C.K., 1953).

   [9]   Hooper, *Bevin*, 3.

appears to have been widely read in the seventeenth and eighteenth centuries and was quoted or commented upon by several writers including Playford, Simpson, Purcell, Hawkins and Burney.

A Briefe and Short Instruction is the only music book known to have been printed by Robert Young, whose business was located 'at the signe of the *Starre* on Bread-street hill'. Young was the owner of the partbook typeface developed by Peter Short and named after him, but he published Bevin's treatise using another font known as the Haultin font. Donald W. Krummel has suggested that Young simply did not know how to use music type and that he subcontracted the printing of Bevin's book to George Wood, another music printer and owner of the Haultin font, even though this font was not used in any books that bear Wood's imprint.[10]

The circumstances of the book's printing may have contributed to typographical problems with the text. Lack of uniformity in font size, spacing, text placement and indentation make it difficult to distinguish between different kinds of text, *e.g.*, headings and labels for musical examples. Also, several in-house corrections are present in most extant copies of the treatise. These issues are addressed in the present edition (see Part II below).

The title page[11] outlines the pedagogical structure of Bevin's treatise (see Figure 1). Comprising 52 pages, it is a 'briefe and short instruction of the art of Musicke'. The opening pages teach students 'how to make Discant, of all proportions [*i.e.*, rhythms] that are in vse'. The following text, 'And may by practice, if they can sing, soone be able to compose three, foure, and five parts', indicates that this book provides instruction on counterpoint, not just elements. Bevin points to his interest in canons when he states 'And also to compose all sorts of Canons that are usuall, by these directions of two or three parts in one, upon the Plain-song'. The bulk of the treatise, from page 7 onwards, is dedicated to examples of different kinds of canonic writing. The contents are as follows:

sig. A4ᵛ	List of consonant and dissonant intervals
pages. 1–4	Examples of different proportions (*i.e.*, rhythms)
pages 5–6	Examples of maintaining a point of imitation
pages 7–23	Two-part canons on plainsong 1 (3 parts total)
pages 24–7	Canons for four and five parts on plainsong 1
pages 28–44	Canons for four and five parts on plainsong 2
pages 45–52	Complex canonic writing for up to 63 parts on plainsong 3

---

[10] Donald W. Krummel, *English Music Printing, 1553–1700* (London: The Biographical Society, 1975), 90–95.

[11] Curiously, the treatise begins on sig. A2 instead of sig. A1.

A
BRIEFE AND
SHORT INSTRVCTI
ON OF THE ART OF

Mvsicke, to teach how to
make Difcant, of all proportions that are in vfe :

VERY NECESSARY FOR ALL
fuch as are defirous to attaine to knowledge in the Art;

And may by practice, if they can fing, foone be able
to compofe three, foure, and five parts : And alfo to compofe all forts of Canons that are ufuall, by thefe directions
of two or three parts in one, upon the Plain-fong.

By ELVVAY BEVIN.

LONDON,

Printed by *R. Young*, at the figne of the *Starre* on Bread-ftreet hill. 1631.

Figure 1   Title Page (sig. A2) of *A Briefe and Short Instruction of the Art of Musicke*. British Library K2.d.14. Used by permission of the British Library and ProQuest Information and Learning Company. Further reproduction is prohibited without permission.

The ordering and the types of canonic writing in Bevin's treatise bring to mind a number of late sixteenth- and early seventeenth-century English manuscript collections of canons written over plainsongs. These may in part be derived from the long and distinguished tradition of plainsong settings by English composers,[12] a tradition that found expression as late as Purcell. In common with *A Briefe and Short Instruction*, the collections assembled by Waterhouse, Bull, Bevin and other mostly anonymous figures involve fairly systematic presentations of canons, with little or no accompanying explanatory text, from two-part examples at different intervals and time distances to more complex examples for three or more parts. Barry Cooper has suggested that by the 1630s the contents of Bevin's treatise were antiquated and belonged to an earlier time.[13] To an extent, this is correct if Bevin's work is regarded as a late representative of the interest in canons written over plainsongs demonstrated by the manuscript collections. However, the references to Bevin by Simpson, Playford and Purcell later in the seventeenth century indicate that the work of the older theorist maintained at least some relevance for later directions in English theory.

An Overview of the Typology of Canons

Bevin's treatise cannot be considered without knowledge of the types of canon in common use. As there is no fully articulated set of terms for canon, it is necessary to provide a combination of modern and historical terms for the different kinds of canonic writing, the procedures and motions employed, and the component parts of a canon. The following discussion attempts to clarify the terms 'canon' and 'canonic writing' and sets out a typology of canon which will be used in the remainder of this study.[14]

As a contrapuntal technique, canon has been associated with strict imitation, starting on the same or a different pitch, of the melodic and rhythmic profile of a given part after a time interval; the imitation may also involve contrary motion, retrograde motion, augmentation, diminution, or a combination. Furthermore, canons can involve restricting the choice of available rhythmic values in a following part. The imitation may last from beginning to end of a piece or it may occur for a section within a piece. Parts with melodic and rhythmic material unrelated to the imitative parts may also be present. Musical puzzles and enigmas are also known

---

[12]   A still useful point of reference is John Caldwell, 'Keyboard Plainsong Settings in England, 1500–1660', *Musica Disciplina* 19 (1965), 129–53.

[13]   Barry Cooper, 'Englische Musiktheorie im 17. und 18. Jahrhundert', in *Entstehung nationaler Traditionen: Frankreich-England. Geschichte der Musiktheorie*, 9 (Darmstadt: Wissenschaftliche Buchgesellschaft, 1986), 164–5.

[14]   A useful general reference for terminology in English sources is Graham Strahle, *An Early Music Dictionary: Musical Terms from British Sources, 1500–1740* (Cambridge: Cambridge University Press, 1995).

as canons, and these are based on the subtle use of musical notation, sometimes accompanied by a short verbal inscription, so that the correct realization of a work poses a challenge. These canons may have nothing to do with imitation, but they involve deriving one or more parts from a given part – a feature in common with imitation canons.[15] Bevin's treatise demonstrates all of these dimensions of canon, and his examples employ canonic writing from beginning to end with no instances of strict imitation alternating with freer kinds of imitative writing.

The phrase 'two parts in one' appears in almost every English theoretical source as equivalent in meaning to two-part canonic imitation. It is defined by Morley as 'when two parts are so made, as one singeth everie note and rest in the same length and order which the leading part did sing before'.[16] Likewise, 'three in one' or 'four in one', etc., are found in English sources. The term 'leading part' is used consistently in the sources in reference to the opening canonic part; however, no term is used to refer to a following part. As there is no term for a straightforward canon by imitation without recourse to devices such as inversion or retrograde motion, in this study I will refer to them as imitation canons in regular motion.[17]

The term *per arsin & thesin* is used for contrary motion imitation in all English sources.[18] *Recte & retro* means that one part takes another part in retrograde motion. 'Double descant' means invertible counterpoint (the latter modern term also embracing double, triple or quadruple counterpoint). English writers refer to a double canon as 'four in two'. This is when two canons are present simultaneously in one composition; for example, a two-part canon at the unison and a two-part canon at the fifth, each based on different melodic and rhythmic material. Likewise triple or quadruple canons may occur, although these are relatively rare in English sources. 'Circle' canons refer to canons that repeat themselves over again until the performers decide to cease, although this term is rarely found in English sources.

Modern scholarship has introduced terms to describe canons for three or more parts involving specialized procedures for which there is no terminology in the historical sources. These terms help to reduce the amount of cumbersome

---

[15]   For much of its history, canon has been associated with the term 'fuga'. This often quite complex relationship is treated in Denis Collins, 'Canon in Music Theory from c. 1550 to c. 1800' (Ph.D. diss., Stanford University, 1992), and in James Haar, 'Zarlino's Definition of Fugue and Imitation', *Journal of the American Musicological Society*, 24 (1971), 226–54.

[16]   Thomas Morley, *A Plaine and Easie Introduction to Practicall Musicke* (London: Peter Short, 1597), 98.

[17]   Sometimes one runs across 'regular' canons or 'direct' canons in the scholarly literature.

[18]   The term 'the point reverted', also encountered in English sources, means inversion of a motif by another part, although the inversion need only last for a few notes. It can occur anywhere during the course of a composition, unlike '*per arsin & thesin*', which involves contrary motion imitation maintained from beginning to end of a piece.

description for procedures that appear to have been standard in canon composition in the sixteenth and seventeenth centuries. 'Stacked' canons involve the same interval of imitation separating successive pairs of voices; for example, a stacked canon at the fifth above means that the second part imitates the first (leading) part at a perfect fifth above, and the third voice imitates the second also at a perfect fifth above. Stacked canons can occur at any interval, although most repertoire examples from the sixteenth, seventeenth and eighteenth centuries are at the fourth or fifth above or below, and a few examples are at the second above.[19] The 'invertible' canon is a canonic subtype in which the original and inverted versions of a two-part canon involving invertible counterpoint at the twelfth are combined to form a three-part composition. First described in the 1573 edition of Zarlino's *Le istitutioni harmoniche*, such canons are frequently encountered in Renaissance music. In the resulting three-part piece, the first and second voices may be in canon at the fifth or fourth (or their compound equivalents) and the second and third voices at the octave, or vice versa.[20]

Canons written over a plainsong abound in English sources from the mid-sixteenth to eighteenth centuries. As used in this study, 'plainsong' canons refer to pieces in which a long-note cantus firmus or plainsong[21] is placed in one part with canonic writing occurring in two or more of the other parts. Non-canonic parts may also be present, and the canonic material is only rarely related to the melodic features of the plainsong. All of the canonic examples in Bevin's treatise are plainsong canons.

'Rounds' and 'catches' are terms that have been used for centuries to describe a canonic structure that is based on a number of equal-length phrases presented successively by each part with imitation at the unison or octave beginning in the following voice when the leading part has completed its first phrase. There are as many phrases as there are parts in the composition, and the opening parts repeat the phrases until the last voice to enter has completed all phrases. Essentially referring to the same musical structure, catches and rounds can set any text, although catches are associated with rude, lewd and scatological expression while rounds usually take pastoral, rustic or religious themes. A variant of this

---

[19] Alan Gosman, 'Stacked Canon and Renaissance Compositional Procedure', *Journal of Music Theory*, 41 (1997), 289–318; David Burn, 'Further Observations on Stacked Canon and Renaissance Compositional Procedure: Gascongne's *Ista est speciosa* and Forestier's *Missa L'homme armé*', *Journal of Music Theory*, 45 (2001), 73–118. Bevin's canon in York Minster Library M.31(s) is an example of a three-part stacked canon at the fifth above.

[20] Invertible canons are described in Peter Schubert, *Modal Counterpoint, Renaissance Style* (New York and Oxford: Oxford University Press, 1999), 216–33.

[21] The terms plainsong and cantus firmus are interchangeable for the purposes of this study. The latter is often associated with a pre-composed liturgical melody, while the former seems to have been understood by English theorists as also including newly composed long-note melodies. I will follow the English sources, which all use the term plainsong rather than cantus firmus.

structure is the 'permutation fugue', found in vocal and instrumental music, where statements of the phrases alternate between tonic and dominant keys. This subtype appears in Purcell's music, although its history has been associated with the music of Bach and his seventeenth-century German predecessors. The term was adapted by Paul Walker from Werner Neumann's 'Permutationsfuge', used in descriptions of J. S. Bach's vocal music.[22]

Another canonic subtype is the canon *per tonos*, a circle canon that repeats itself transposed up or down a whole tone, passing through different modal or tonal centres until the music returns to its starting pitch (up or down an octave). Canons *per tonos* are found from Willaert onwards, with occasional examples repeating their material at other intervals, usually the fifth.[23] Examples are included in many treatise accounts of canon, including those by Morley and Simpson, who use the term 'canon rising or falling a note'; otherwise, there is no term for this procedure until Marpurg coined 'canon *per tonos*' in the 1750s. The best-known repertoire example is the canon *per tonos* from J. S. Bach's *Musical Offering*.

A very useful term, possibly coined by Bevin, occurs uniquely in British Library RM 24.c.14. The 'duplex' canon refers to a three- or four-part canon in which the second part imitates the leading part in contrary motion and the third part imitates the leading part in regular motion. If a fourth part is present, it imitates the leading part in contrary motion. The intervals of imitation are usually the unison or octave; that is, the second part may enter with imitation at the unison and the third part at the octave, or vice versa. Time distances separating the voice entries may be equal or unequal. Many duplex canons are found in manuscript plainsong collections attributed to Bevin and Bull (British Library RM 24.c.14 and Österreichische Nationalbibliothek Mus. Hs. 17.771 respectively).

A term introduced in this study is the 'parallel' canon. This involves the second part imitating the first at the perfect fourth or fifth and the third part imitating the first at the octave. If a fourth part is present it imitates the second part at the octave. Thus, an imitating part parallels another part at the distance of an octave. In such canons the imitation between all of the parts is either above or below (never mixed); for instance, a parallel canon at the fifth, octave and twelfth below means that a soprano part is imitated by the alto at the fifth below, and then a tenor imitates at an octave below the soprano, and finally the bass enters at the twelfth below the soprano (that is, an octave below the alto). Parallel canons are perhaps the most commonly encountered three- and four-part canonic subtypes in sixteenth- and seventeenth-century music. Although parallel canons are not

---

[22]   Paul Walker, 'The Origin of the Permutation Fugue', in *The Creative Process. Studies in the History of Music*, 3 (New York: Broude Bros. Ltd., 1992), 51–91.

[23]   Edward E. Lowinsky, 'Music in Titian's *Bacchanal of the Andrians*: Origins and History of the *canon per tonos*', in *Music and Culture of the Renaissance and Other Essays*, 2 vols., ed. Bonnie J. Blackburn (Chicago: University of Chicago Press, 1989), i, 298–350. Terms such as 'modulating canons' and 'spiral canons' are occasionally used by other scholars for this procedure.

included in Bevin's treatise, there are numerous examples of them in English theoretical and repertoire sources, including the manuscript collection attributed to Bevin (British Library RM 24.c.14). They will therefore be included in the following discussion.

English Theories of Canon before Bevin

Canonic writing is considered in a small number of sixteenth- and early seventeenth-century English treatises.[24] An anonymous sixteenth-century Scottish manuscript has an extensive section on verbal inscriptions associated with puzzle canons but nothing on imitative canonic writing.[25] Substantial sections dealing with canon are found in William Bathe's *A Briefe Introduction to the Skill of Song* (1596)[26] and Thomas Morley's *A Plaine and Easie Introduction to Practicall Musicke* (1597). Some material on imitative counterpoint is found in Giovanni Coprario's *Rules How to Compose* (1610) but there is nothing on canon.[27]

In *A Briefe Introduction to the Skill of Song*, William Bathe provides a numerical table for composing two-part canons over a plainsong according to a combinatorial method. By referring to the table, a student can decide on a note for the leading part that not only forms a consonant interval with a plainsong note but will also lead to a consonant interval between the second canonic part and the next plainsong note. The method can work for any plainsong chosen by the aspiring composer of canons. An admirably clear and detailed explanation of how to use Bathe's table and accompanying instructions is given by Kevin C. Karnes in his critical edition of this treatise.[28]

---

[24] A good introduction to English theory of this period may be found in Jessie Ann Owens, 'Concepts of Pitch in English Music Theory, c. 1560–1640,' in *Tonal Structures in Early Music*, ed. Cristle Collins Judd (New York and London: Garland, 1998), 183–246. Useful overviews of English contrapuntal theory are in Lillian M. Ruff, 'The Seventeenth-Century English Music Theorists' (Ph.D. diss., University of Nottingham, 1962); Barry Cooper, 'Englische Musiktheorie im 17. und 18. Jahrhundert'; and Rebecca Herissone, *Music Theory in Seventeenth-Century England* (Oxford: Oxford University Press, 2000).

[25] See Judson Dana Maynard, 'An Anonymous Scottish Treatise on Music from the Sixteenth Century, British Museum, Additional Manuscript 4911. Edition and Commentary' (Ph.D. diss., Indiana University, 1961).

[26] The publication history of Bathe's treatise is described in William Bathe, *A Briefe Introduction to the Skill of Song*, ed. Kevin C. Karnes (Aldershot: Ashgate, 2005), 3–15.

[27] A modern edition of this treatise is in *A New Way of Making Fowre Parts in Counterpoint by Thomas Campion and Rules how to Compose by Giovanni Coprario*, ed. Christopher R. Wilson (Aldershot: Ashgate, 2003).

[28] Bathe, *A Briefe Introduction*, ed. Karnes, 32–42, 72–81. Bathe's table is reproduced on p. 36 of Karnes's edition. The illustration of a 'Musical Sword' (*Gladius Musicus*) in Bathe's text to obtain results identical to the table when composing 'two parts in one' is described in note 38, pp. 96–7.

Bathe's instructions pertain to consonant harmonic intervals formed between each canonic voice and the plainsong on the onset of each note of the plainsong, and the temporal distance between the parts is the same as the rhythmic note value of the plainsong (*e.g.*, a semibreve) or a multiple of it. As such, Bathe is providing a guide for constructing note-against-note versions of canons, and he does not offer any guidelines for how the student should proceed to finished versions. It is possible that the '10. sundry waies of 2. parts in one vpon the plain song' at the end of Bathe's treatise were meant to be studied by the student for guidance in this respect.[29] However, in several of these canons the interval of imitation is at the eleventh or twelfth above or below with the plainsong occupying the middle register, whereas Bathe's table deals only with intervals of imitation from unison to octave above or below, and it seems to assume that the plainsong will always be the lowest of the three parts present. It is possible that compound intervals are assumed by Bathe for intervals of imitation between the canonic parts and also for the permitted harmonic intervals formed between the plainsong and each of the canonic parts.

One very useful feature of Bathe's table is that it includes information about which melodic intervals in the leading part will lead to errors in part-writing such as parallel fifths and octaves or unwanted dissonances even in those cases where a consonant harmonic interval between leading part and plainsong has been selected from the table.[30] Consequently, there are two types of information provided by Bathe's table. The first relates to the consonant harmonic intervals between the leading part and plainsong that will lead to consonant intervals between the next plainsong note and the note that appears by imitation in the second canonic part. This three-way relationship between all voices in the texture is what makes plainsong canon composition particularly challenging. The second type of information pertains to all two-part imitation canons whether or not a plainsong is present: the leading part's melodic intervals formed by notes separated by the temporal distance of the canon must not lead to dissonances when the following voice imitates at the same or different pitches (*i.e.*, unison or non-unison canons).

These issues were also considered by the sixteenth-century Italian theorists Lusitano, Vicentino, Zarlino and Tigrini, with the most thorough-going exposition provided by Zarlino in the revised 1573 edition of *Le istitutioni harmoniche*.[31] It is

---

[29]   Bathe, *A Briefe Introduction*, ed. Karnes, 85–90.

[30]   This matter is treated fully by Karnes on pp. 41–2 of his edition.

[31]   Vicente Lusitano, *Introduttione facilissima et novissima di canto fermo, figurato, contraponto semplice, et in concerto* (Rome [no publisher], 1553), sigs. C4–E4. Nicola Vicentino, *L'antica musica ridotta alla moderna prattica* (Rome: Antonio Barre, 1555; facs. ed. E. Lowinsky, Kassel: Bäreneiter, 1959), fol. 83. Gioseffo Zarlino, *Le istitutioni harmoniche*, 3rd edn (Venice: F. Senese, 1573), 302–17. Oratio Tigrini, *Il compendiolo della musica* (Venice: Ricciardo Amadino, 1588; facs. edn New York: Broude Bros., 1966), 116–20. A detailed discussion of these sources is in Ernest T. Ferand, 'Improvised Vocal

difficult to say if Bathe was familiar with Zarlino's 1573 edition of *Le istitutioni harmoniche*; it is quite possible that he devised his table independently, and the use of his own somewhat idiosyncratic terminology may support this possibility. However, Bathe's terminology and some unfortunate and potentially disorienting typographical errors and inconsistencies in punctuation render his discussion of canonic composition rather opaque. This lack of clarity and directness may have hindered the treatise's reception amongst writers interested in imitative contrapuntal procedures. Furthermore, Karnes suggests that despite its novelty, his method may not have been considered an improvement over existing teaching practices because a student using Bathe's table would need conscientiously to check and continually adjust the unfolding canonic texture.[32]

The likely date of publication of Bathe's treatise was 1596, and it is therefore difficult to say with certainty if it was known to Morley, whose *Introduction* was published the following year.[33] Bathe's treatise appears not to have engaged later English writers, whereas Morley's treatise, in contrast, was one of the most widely read and influential books about music published in England. Morley's material on canon is an ad hoc assembly of discussion, observations and examples of canonic writing that stands in contrast to Bathe's terse exposition of a method of canonic writing. The claim that 'the forme of making the *Canons* is so manie and diuers waies altered, that no generall rule may be gathered',[34] made at the outset of Morley's discussion of canons in the second part of the treatise, suggests that he was not familiar with Bathe's tabular scheme for writing canons.

The issue of how much of Morley's discussion of contrapuntal techniques is uniquely his own and how much is derived from other sources, especially Italian treatises, is troublesome. Many passages are clearly derived from Zarlino; for instance, the section on invertible counterpoint reads almost exactly like Zarlino's chapter on invertible counterpoint but with Morley's own examples.[35] Comments and questions from the student Philomathes are noticeably absent from this section of the text. Another passage recalling Zarlino is how canons can be notated as one line of music from which other parts are derived.[36] However, Morley steers clear of Zarlino's terminological complexities, in which canonic writing is considered as a type of *fuga* or *imitatione* depending on whether exact intervallic correspondence is maintained between the imitating parts.[37] This may reflect the

---

Counterpoint in the Late Renaissance and Early Baroque', *Annales Musicologiques*, 4 (1956), 129–74. See also Denis Collins, 'Zarlino and Berardi as Teachers of Canon', *Theoria*, 7 (1993), 103–23.

[32] Bathe, *A Briefe Introduction*, ed. Karnes, 43–4.

[33] Jessie Ann Owens suggests that Morley's explanation of the gamut, particularly the words in italic font, may have been drawn word by word from Bathe's treatise. See Owens, 'Concepts of Pitch', 200–201.

[34] Morley, *Introduction*, 98.

[35] Morley, *Introduction*, 105–15.

[36] Ibid., 104–5.

[37] See Haar, 'Zarlino's Definition of Fugue and Imitation'.

orientation of English theory towards teaching beginners the art of singing and elementary counterpoint with little attention to speculative discussion.[38] Morley's discussion of canon is based much more upon plainsong canons than Zarlino's, and this may in part result from the great interest in plainsong canons among English musicians towards the end of the sixteenth century. Morley's principal contributions to canonic theory may be seen in two areas: the presentation of a series of plainsong canons aimed at a beginning student and the inclusion of a canon *per arsin & thesin* by William Byrd.

The student Philomathes was apparently expected to learn from the musical examples many details about canonic writing not mentioned in the Master's text. Philomathes provides two of the twelve examples of two-part plainsong canons that form the central part of Morley's exposition on canon.[39] All of these examples, apart from the first two, are based on a plainsong that Morley appears to have created for the purpose of his discussion of canon. This plainsong was also used by Bevin for the examples on pp. 28–44 of his treatise, and it is also found in the manuscript collection of plainsong canons associated with Bevin, British Library RM 24.c.14. The first three examples – two by the Master and one by Philomathes – are given in two forms, 'plaine' and 'diuided'. The plain version is a note-against-note framework upon which the divided version is derived by means of varying the rhythms with repeated notes, passing notes or suspensions. Having two versions of an example is a useful pedagogical tool as it permits the student Philomathes to understand the harmonic intervallic relationships between the three voices in the canonic texture, although the Master does not state this explicitly.[40] This approach may indicate how Morley and his contemporaries went about writing canons, or at least how students began their study of canon. The plain version also corresponds to what a student would come up with when following Bathe's instructions.

Although Morley does not provide systematic instruction on how the leading part is constructed in the presence of a plainsong in order to arrive at a plain version of a canon, he does give specific rules for writing canons at the fourth and fifth. The placement of these rules is potentially disorienting for the reader because they come immediately after the statement that 'no generall rule may be gathered' for writing canons.

---

[38]   Owens, 'Concepts of Pitch', 189.

[39]   Morley does not provide instruction for writing canons with more than two imitating parts. He mentions on p. 115 that 'as for foure partes in tvvo, sixe in three, and such like, you may hereafter make them vpon a plainsong, when you shall haue learned to make them without it'.

[40]   Modern transcriptions of the examples can be found in Thomas Morley, *A Plain and Easy Introduction to Practical Music*, ed. R. Alec Harman (New York: W. W. Norton, 1952). Harman's edition occasionally substitutes the word 'imitation' for Morley's 'fuge'.

[Y]et in the making of two parts in one in the fourth, if you would haue your following part in the waie of counterpoint to follow within one note after the other, you must not ascend two, nor descend three. But if you descend two, and ascend three, it wil be well.

And by the contrarie in two partes in one in the fift, you may go as manie downe together as you will, but not vp.[41]

The first rule is followed by a canon at the fourth above (see Examples 1a and 1b), and the second is followed by a canon at the fifth above (see Examples 2a and 2b), each in plain and divided form. These rules may have been deduced from Bathe's instructions, but Morley's understanding of them is suspect because he makes no mention of stepwise motion or of intervals of a fifth or larger in the leading part in canons at the fourth, and his rule for canons at the fifth is very unclear.[42]

Example 1a   Morley, canon at the fourth above, 'plaine' version. *Introduction*, 98

---

[41]   Both comments occur in Morley, *Introduction*, 98–99. In a canon at the fourth above after a semibreve the note onsets that are separated by semibreves in the leading part must not form the interval of an ascending third or a descending fourth because they will clash with the notes of the following part entering at the fourth above (leading to a second or seventh respectively). A descending third or ascending fourth in the leading part will work well with the following part (leading to a sixth or unison respectively). His prescription for a canon at the fifth is muddled because not all descending intervals in the leading part will lead to consonances with the following part (*i.e.*, the permitted intervals are the unison, descending second, fourth and sixth, and ascending third and fifth).

[42]   Morley's words 'go as manie downe together as you will, but not vp' may mean that one or more descending seconds in the leading voice will work but ascending seconds will not. This interpretation agrees with that found in Julian Grimshaw, 'Morley's Rule for First-Species Canon', *Early* Music, 34 (2006), 661–6. Perhaps to illustrate this, Example 2a contains a series of descending seconds between bars 3 and 5, while the opening bars have ascending thirds followed by a descending fourth giving a short sequence in the leading voice in bars 2 and 3 that is emphasized in the divided version, Example 2b.

Example 1b   Morley, canon at the fourth above, 'diuided' version.
Introduction, 98

The 'plaine' version of the canon at the fourth above (Example 1a) is essentially a first-species exercise showing how the canonic voices can proceed by permitted intervals. The 'diuided' version (Example 1b) shows how the same notes mostly occur at the beginning of each semibreve unit in the canonic parts, thus ensuring maintenance of the overall consonant framework, with repeated notes, passing notes, rests, and the 'fake'[43] fourth-species suspension formula (in the second and final bars) filling out the texture. In the second half of bar 3 and the first half of bar 4 the leading part substitutes different notes on the first minims, each of which fortunately leads to consonances with both the following part and the plainsong a semibreve later. This rather subtle manoeuvre requires careful study by the beginning student of canon and is an instance of where details of the compositional craft must be gleaned from the examples rather than from the accompanying text. Fourths occur between the two canonic parts in bars 3 and 4 (see Example 1b), but potential voice-leading problems are avoided because of the intervals formed between the plainsong and the leading part, the two lowest parts in the example. Morley does not comment on this useful means of allowing fourths between the two upper parts in plainsong canons (where the plainsong is the lowest part). The descending fifths in bars 5 and 6 are filled in by stepwise motion, a popular device in many canonic examples from the period.

Morley's second example, also in plain and divided forms, shows how the plainsong may be converted to a free part that participates in the imitative texture: its opening phrase is very similar in contour to the canonic melody, it forms

---

[43]   Peter Schubert describes the 'fake' suspension as when the dissonance is not prepared correctly, in *Modal Counterpoint, Renaissance Style*, 75.

parallel thirds or tenths with the upper parts in several places, and it maintains rhythmic interest in bars 4, 5 and 6 where the upper parts have semibreves (see Examples 2a and 2b). Morley says that he has 'broken the plainsong of purpose, and caused it to answer in Fuge as a third part to the others'.[44] This leads to what looks like a tonal answer between the lower two voices, although this is undercut by the entry of the second canonic voice and perhaps also by the overall modal flavour of the piece concluding with a typical renaissance cadence with a major sixth between the outer two parts expanding to an octave.

Example 2a   Morley, canon at the fifth above, 'plaine' version. *Introduction*, 99

Example 2b   Morley, canon at the fifth above, 'diuided' version. *Introduction*, 99

Other aspects of this example that Morley may have expected the student to notice during careful study include the leap of a fourth in the penultimate bar,

---

[44]   Morley, *Introduction*, 99.

which would normally lead to an unwanted dissonance but is treated here by a cadential 4–3 suspension formula. Also, Philomathes may have been expected to observe the frequent use of parallel motion between the plainsong and leading part and the adjustment to the plainsong in bar 4 to avoid parallel fifths in the plain version.

The next example, by Philomathes, is at the fifth below and is the last example to be presented in plain and divided forms (Examples 3a and 3b). The number of fourths between the canonic parts shows that Philomathes has learned how this interval may be handled correctly when the plainsong is the lowest part. The leading voice moves mainly by step with some instances of parallel motion with the plainsong. The divided version is quite accomplished with two points of imitation and the beginning of a third carved from the plain version. Rests separate each point and suspensions provide additional interest to the texture. In like manner Philomathes next offers a canon at the fourth above in divided form only with two points of imitation.[45] This example follows Morley's earlier recommendations about avoiding an ascending third or descending fourth but allowing a descending third or ascending fourth.

There next follows a group of eight canons, three of which are at the fifth[46] and followed by one each at intervals from the sixth to tenth. They employ time distances of a minim, semibreve and breve, whereas the previous examples were all at the semibreve. Morley says that 'they be done by plaine sight without rule', meaning that there is little guidance to offer the student except practice and study of examples.[47] Consequently, Morley does not discuss these examples. The presence of so many canons at the fifth (five so far) and fourth (two so far) suggests that Morley may have considered these the most commonly used intervals in canonic writing. The student is left to study the significance of what is involved when imitation occurs at time distances apart from a semibreve. This is one area where Morley could have given some practical advice; for instance, in a canon at a minim distance, the 'plaine' version would need to have minims rather than semibreves, whereas at a breve distance it does not necessarily follow that the plain version would involve a reduction of the canonic parts to breves (because the plainsong moves by semibreves). Morley seems to assume that by 'plaine sight' the student would be able to gauge which melodic progressions in the leading part would maintain a consonant framework with the following part and with the next melodic note of the plainsong. Another feature of the canons presented

---

[45]   Morley, *Introduction*, 100.

[46]   Morley, *Introduction*, 100–103. One of them is at the twelfth below even though Morley refers to it as at the fifth. In most cases the plainsong is in the lowest part; exceptions are the top part in one of the canons at the fifth and the middle part in the canon at the twelfth.

[47]   The phrase 'plaine sight' is encountered frequently in English sources dealing with canon. It seems to mean that the student should work through the canonic exercise without any prior precepts for guidance.

Example 3a   Morley, canon at the fifth below, 'plaine' version. *Introduction,*
99

Example 3b   Morley, canon at the fifth below, 'diuided' version. *Introduction,*
100

in these pages is the use of a repeated rhythmic idea or of motifs (the same one
or different ones) occurring two or three times, sometimes with entries preceded
by rests. The repetition of the opening G–C fourth in bar 3 of the plainsong is
exploited to this purpose, as demonstrated by the canon at the fifth above after
a minim with the plainsong in the lowest part (Example 4).

So far all of the canons have employed imitation in regular motion. Another
category is one 'which the maisters call *per arsin & thesin*, that is by rising and
falling, for when the higher part ascendeth, the lower descendeth, and when the
lower part ascendeth, the higher parte descendeth', and it can take place at any
interval of imitation between the parts.[48] Two examples are presented, the first of
which is short and is notable for breaking the strict contrary motion imitation by

---

[48]   Morley, p. 102. His examples and discussion follow on pp. 103–4.

Example 4   Morley, canon at the fifth above. *Introduction,* 101

placing a semibreve rest in the following part that does not occur in the leading part.[49] The second example is by William Byrd (see Example 5):

> which for difficultie in the composition is not inferior to anie which I haue seen ... which thing, how hard it is to performe vpon a plainsong, none can perfectlie know, but hee who hath or shal go about to doe the like ... But in my opinion, who soeuer shal go about to make such another, vpon anie common knowne plainsong or hymne, shal find more difficultie then he looked for.[50]

Morley gives no practical advice to Philomathes on how to write a piece of this type. He apparently believes that there are no rules available to assist the student and that 'plaine sight' is required to maintain consonances among the parts and to create a pleasing divided texture. Morley's only comment – 'to speake vprightlie, I take the plainsong to bee made with the descant, for the more easie effecting of his purpose', – indicates that the plainsong was composed simultaneously with the other parts in order to make the task more manageable.

Aspects of this canon that Philomathes may have been expected to observe through careful study include the ingenious use of points of imitation and their

---

[49]   Transcription in Harman, p. 185. The additional semibreve rest is not commented on by Morley (or Harman).

[50]   This canon is included in the Byrd edition as one of only two canons that may be confidently attributed to Byrd. See the *Byrd Edition* 16: Madrigals, Songs and Canons, ed. Philip Brett (London: Stainer and Bell, 1976), 169–70. The preface to the edition outlines the editor's reasons for excluding various other canons once attributed to Byrd; much of this material also appeared in Brett, 'Did Byrd Write "Non nobis, Domine"?', *Musical Times*, 113/1555 (1972), 855–7. Brett's transcription retains the original clefs, whereas Harman's edition (pp. 185–6) replaces the original C clefs with transposing treble clefs. The transcription in Example 5 is my own.

Example 5   Byrd canon in Morley, *Introduction*, 103–4

inversions such that it may be difficult to perceive which voice assumes the role of leading part at any one time. The entry of the second part in bar 2 becomes the material for the leading part in bar 3, while the notes that appeared in the leading part in bar 1 return in the following part in bar 4. Such skilful manipulation of melodic material is possible by using inversion at the twelfth where the notes A and E (the opening notes of the leading and following parts) invert to become each other. Therefore, Byrd can present seamless interactions of melodic ideas throughout the piece, as in the treatment of a variation of the motif beginning in bar 6 which leads to what is almost an echo effect towards the end of the piece. The texture is further enriched by the free part, which from bar 7 onward is based on the material in the canonic voices.

Byrd's example shows how the use of points of imitation in the earlier example provided by Philomathes (Example 3b above) can be worked to great effect by an accomplished master. Philomathes may also have made the more humble observation that the use of rests could simplify the task of writing a canon *per arsin & thesin* (although they also serve the purpose of articulating the voice entries), and he may have noticed further that when the canonic parts are heard together they are frequently in parallel motion, especially in the opening bars of the piece.[51]

In the third part of the *Introduction*, Morley surveys briefly some subtypes of canon.[52] He quotes a puzzle canon from Josquin's *Missa Fortuna desperata* and observes that 'though this be no Canon in that sence as wee commonly take it, as not being more parts in one, yet be these words a *Canon*'. For the other parts he directs the student to Glarean's *Dodecachordon*. Morley also considers a puzzle canon from the Kyrie of Pierre de la Rue's *Missa O salutaris hostia* in which a single notated line of music has letters and fermata signs above certain notes indicating where the other parts enter and conclude. Not to be outdone, Morley presents his own musical puzzle, a piece notated in the form of a cross 'which is indeed so obscure that no man without the Resolution wil find out how it may be sung'. Fortunately, Morley explains how to arrive at the solution and notates all of the parts.[53] Next follows a short example of a canon *per tonos*, although Morley does not give it any name. His example is very short and gives the first three statements beginning on D, C and B flat with remaining statements presumably completing the whole-tone progression downwards until the piece concludes on D. Morley provides guidelines for writing a canon *recte & retro* for eight parts: start with a four-part piece for two pairs of equal voices, then

---

[51]   Morley acknowledges the value of Byrd's example and claims that 'whosoeuer will exercise himselfe diligentlie in that kinde, may in short time become an excellent Musician, because that he vvho in it is perfect, may almost at the first sight see what may be done vpon anie plainsong'. *Introduction*, 114–15.

[52]   *Introduction*, 173–7.

[53]   Reproduced in facsimile in Herissone, *Music Theory in Seventeenth-Century England*, 201, plate 7.1.

join the retrograde of one voice to the end of its partner so that an eight-part piece results. He refers the student to an unnamed eight-part example by Byrd.[54] Morley's brief mention of the catch is supported by an example notated in two ways: as a four-part piece written in score format and a resolution in which each performer sings all four parts in succession.

In summary, Morley gives an overview of various aspects of canon including terminology, notation, intervals of imitation, the application of contrary motion, retrograde motion and invertible counterpoint, and a brief survey of puzzle canons. The text does not provide a well-structured introduction to canonic writing, but Morley's pedagogical intention is manifest through the student Philomathes's comments, questions and contributions of student exercises. Many details about writing plainsong canons can only be ascertained from careful perusal of the examples, although it is not clear to what extent Morley intended this process to be part of his teaching method. However, study of the examples is very useful given the paucity of written instruction on canonic writing in historical sources.[55] Nothing further on canon is found in English writings of the first decades of the seventeenth century until Bevin's treatise.

Collections of Plainsong Canons

The keen interest among late sixteenth- and early seventeenth-century English musicians in the technical challenges of writing a series of plainsong canons for two or more parts is evident in a number of manuscript and printed collections. This interest arose in part from the context of music training where students learned improvisation over a plainsong before progressing to instruction in plainsong-based compositional techniques.[56] Extensive study of short pieces demonstrating aspects of compositional technique was expected of students and examples were provided by their masters. Plainsong canons, exercises in invertible counterpoint and musical puzzles were a natural consequence of this process, and were well provided for by many composers, leading in some cases to an obsession with working out the canonic potential of a chosen plainsong. It is possible that an element of prestige may have been associated with demonstrated proficiency in writing canons. A requirement for the doctoral degree in music at

---

[54] This piece is *Diliges Dominum*. A modern edition is in the *Byrd Edition*, vol. 1: *Cantiones sacrae (1575)*, ed. Craig Monson (London: Stainer and Bell, 1977), 151–60.

[55] Herissone, *Music Theory in Seventeenth-Century England*, 194, points out that theorists typically did not discuss larger-scale organization of musical works; therefore it is perhaps not surprising that little detailed instruction on how to compose canons is found in treatises.

[56] See Jane Flynn, 'The Education of Choristers in England during the Sixteenth Century', in *English Choral Practice 1400–1650*, ed. John Morehen (Cambridge: Cambridge University Press, 1995), 180–99.

Oxford University included canonic composition, and the principal contributors to the canonic repertoire – Byrd, Bull, Bevin, Farmer and Waterhouse – were all associated with the Chapel Royal.[57] On a more mundane level, Fellowes suggested that connoisseurs of canon 'no doubt took delight in constructing something which might baffle a rival musician in his attempts at finding the solution'.[58]

Plainsong canon collections stand apart from repertoire examples and theoretical writings because of their dedication towards exhaustive exploration of a particular aspect of compositional technique, resulting in dozens or even hundreds of pieces possibly only intended for private study or circulation among interested experts. Only Farmer's set of 40 plainsong canons resulted in publication, and this is one of the shortest of the collections. These collections lie somewhere between the domains of music treatises and composition as they provide systematic treatment of the topic of plainsong canon by way of examples but without accompanying explanatory text. The collections were assembled towards the end of the sixteenth and beginning of the seventeenth centuries, and they arguably represent the point of greatest interest in canonic technique among English musicians. Bevin's treatise probably arose from this climate, although it had a relatively late date of publication in 1631 when Bevin was towards the end of his career. Table 1 lists plainsong canon collections with brief descriptions of their contents and authorship, where known.

Certain plainsongs appeared to have been especially attractive vehicles for demonstrations of technical display, with the *Miserere* melody stimulating the most extensive and exhaustive contrapuntal activity.[59] Bevin also used this plainsong for the last group of canons in his treatise. Circulation of plainsong canons among Elizabethan musicians is suggested by Morley, who refers to a friendly competition between Byrd and Ferrabosco the Younger in writing canons on *Miserere*: 'vvich caused them striue euerie one to surmount another, vvithout malice, enuie, or backbiting: but by great labour, studie and paines, ech making other censure of that which they had done'.[60] The results of this competition were never published, although it has long been thought that one was intended.[61]

---

[57] This point is made in Peter Kolb Danner, 'The Miserere Mihi and the English Reformation: A Study of the Evolution of a Cantus Firmus Genre in Tudor Music' (Ph.D. diss., Stanford University, 1967), 114.

[58] Edmund H. Fellowes, *William Byrd*, 2nd edn (London: Oxford University Press, 1948), 173.

[59] Occasional settings of the *Miserere* melody involving canonic imitation may also be found in the English repertoire. One example is a keyboard work by John Lugge (1580–?), in John Lugge, *Complete Keyboard Works*, ed. Susi Jeans and John Steele (London: Novello, 1990), 2–4.

[60] Morley, *Introduction*, 115.

[61] Fellowes, *Byrd*, 173–4. Fellowes suggested an intended date of 1603 under the title *Medulla Musicke* but that the project was stopped by Byrd and Ferrabosco because it would have involved arrangements of the canons by one Thomas Robinson.

Table 1   Plainsong canon collections

Source	Contents	Attribution/Date
British Library Add. 31391	29 canons. 19 on *Miserere*	'W.B.' Late 16th century
British Library Add. 29996	40 canons. *Miserere*	'Tho. Woodson'. Late 16th century
British Library RM 24.c.14y	300 canons. Most on *Miserere*	Elway Bevin. 17th century
British Library RM 24.f.25	24 canons. 13 on *Miserere*	John Bull (et al.). 18th-century copy
Österreichische Nationalbibliothek Mus. Hs. 17.771	126 canons. *Miserere*	John Bull. 17th century
Cambridge University Library Dd.iv.60	1163 canons. *Miserere*	George Waterhouse
British Library RM 24.d.7	'W.B.' canons 40 canons. (Other misc. vocal music)	John Farmer (published 1591) 18th-century copy
British Library RM 24.d.12	12 non-canonic bicinia 9 short unison canons 99 canons on *Laudate Dominum* 'W.B.' canons'	'Orlandus Lassus, Belga' Anonymous 'Don Ferdinandi' [= Fernando de las Infantas] 18th-century copy

Edmund Fellowes believed that some of Byrd's canons made their way into British Library Add. 31391, a contemporary vellum-bound manuscript with the initials W.B. placed after each of 29 canons. However, Byrd's authorship of the canons in this source has been resolutely dismissed by Philip Brett on the basis of no resemblance to Byrd's established canonic output and the prevalence of technical solecisms and awkward part-writing.[62] Most of these 29 what may be called pseudo-Byrd canons involve two- or three-part imitation over one of three plainsongs (*O lux beata Trinitas* in the first five, *Per naturam* in nos. 6–10 and *Miserere* in the remainder). Procedures such as augmentation, contrary motion and retrograde motion appear in several of the pieces. Unprepared or incorrectly resolved dissonances abound, as do 6/4 sonorities, angular melodic lines and various vertical note arrangements that defy description. Several non-imitative puzzle canons have fewer errors than the pieces employing canonic imitation. For example, canon 8 is solved by the second canonic part singing the notes of

---

[62]   Brett, 'Did Byrd Write "Non nobis, Domine"?'

the leading part as semibreves only. The solution to no. 14, involving rearranging the notes of the given line from largest to smallest rhythmic values, was unknown until solved by Hans T. David and printed in Fellowes's book.[63] Solutions to the other canons have exercised various minds over the centuries and can be found in two eighteenth-century manuscripts in the British Library, RM 24.d.7 and RM 24.d.12.

Included in British Library RM 24.d.12 are three other contrapuntal sets. The first is headed by the words 'Orlandus Lassus, Belga' and is a group of 12 non-canonic bicinia.[64] A group of nine canons follows for three, four or eight parts. These are nothing more than short exercises in elementary imitation. A more substantial collection of 99 pieces over the melody *Laudate Dominum omnes gentes* explores canonic and non-canonic imitation for two to seven parts at various intervals and time distances. Fol. 16 has the text 'Hic terminantur ea, quae facta fuerunt ab auctore in suis principiis. Contra puncta Don Ferdinandi', and the top of the next page has 'et sequuntur quae addita fuerunt (ut amicis morem gererit) A. 1571'.[65] These canons are by Fernando de las Infantas and were published in his *Plura modulationum genera* (Venice, 1579). Given that this manuscript is a copy dating from the eighteenth century, it is not possible to judge the extent to which its contents were known to late sixteenth- or early seventeenth-century English musicians.

British Library RM 24.d.7 contains the set of 40 canons by John Farmer that were published in 1591 by Thomas East.[66] These are all based on a plainsong derived from the second phrase of a Sarum version of the Kyrie *Cunctipotens genitor Deus*.[67] This publication includes comments of a general nature for some of the canons similar to the comments found in Bevin's treatise. The canons, at intervals from unison to tenth, are of mixed quality with many containing part-writing errors and others resembling little more than exercises in first- or

---

[63]   Fellowes, *Byrd*, 176.

[64]   For a modern edition of these pieces see Orlando di Lasso, *The Complete Motets*, vol. 11, ed. Peter Bergquist (Madison: A-R Editions, 1995). Wolfgang Boetticher states that the source for the duos in this manuscript was Lasso's 1577 *Novae aliquot, ad duas voces cantiones* (Munich: Adam Berg). See Wolfgang Boetticher, *Orlando di Lasso und seine Zeit* (Bärenreiter, 1958; expanded reissue, Wilhelmshaven: Florian Noetzel, 1999), 827.

[65]   'Here end those which were made by the author in his Principles. Counterpoints of Don Ferdinand. ... and [now] follow the additional points that have been added (so that he has produced a model for his friends) A[nno Domini] 1571'. 'Principia' was commonly used in titles of learned works from antiquity to the seventeenth century. 'Morem' can refer to a doctrine or a philosophy.

[66]   John Farmer, *Divers & Sundry Waies of Two Parts in One, to the Number of Fortie vppon one Playnsong* (London: Thomas East, 1591). The canons have been transcribed in Lewis P. Bowling, 'A Transcription and Comparative Analysis of Divers and Sundry Waies of Two Parts in One (1591) by John Farmer' (D.A. diss., University of Northern Colorado, 1982). The transcriptions that appear in the present discussion are my own.

[67]   Bowling, *Comparative Analysis*, 27–8.

second-species counterpoint. More successful results are demonstrated by canon 4 (Example 6), which is at the twelfth above with the plainsong in the middle register. The melodic lines are stately, the rhythmic balance between the parts is well handled, and the Dorian modality is brightened by is brightened by a shift to G in bars 6-7.

Example 6   Farmer, Canon 4, *Divers and Sundry Waies*

More challenging is canon 34 (canon 35 in the manuscript numbering) at the tenth below after a semibreve with the plainsong in the highest part (Example 7). Farmer's remark that 'this is a verie difficult way to make' is reflected in the static melodic lines and frequent rests. The difficulty arises in the preponderance of stepwise movement in the plainsong, which restricts the available choice of notes in the leading part in a canon at this interval. For instance, in bars 1–2, D is the only consonant note available to the leading part against the plainsong A because any other note will lead to a dissonance with the following part when the plainsong descends by step to G.

Example 7   Farmer, Canon 34, *Divers and Sundry Waies*

The puzzle canons in Farmer's collection involve many of the procedures found in other collections and in Bevin's treatise, namely, contrary motion, retrograde motion involving the plainsong or one of the canonic voices, contrary motion and retrograde motion together, or imitation involving rhythmic alteration (*e.g.*, canon 13, where the second canonic part moves entirely by minims). Farmer's publication resembles Bevin's treatise most especially in the presentation of canonic examples with no explanatory text but with occasional remarks about the ordering of voices and the difficulties involved in certain pieces.

On fol. 184^v of the British Library manuscript Add. 29996 the words 'Forty Wayes of 2 pts in one: of Tho. Woodson' are placed before a group of only 20 canons based on the plainsong *Miserere*. These canons, discussed in detail with six transcriptions by Hugh Miller,[68] involve imitation at intervals from unison to thirteenth at time distances of up to three semibreves. Imitation by augmentation is used in canon 1, while canons 2, 9 and 20 involve the kind of rhythmic alteration encountered in other collections, *i.e.*, one part moves consistently in semibreves while the other canonic part has the same melody but rhythmically varied.

This manuscript has other canons at various places: a group of 16 anonymous pieces entitled 'Pretty Wayes: for young beginners to looke on' (fols. 192^v, 193^r,

---

[68]   Hugh M. Miller, 'Forty Wayes of 2 pts. In One of Tho[mas] Woodson', *Journal of the American Musicological Society*, 8 (1955), 14–21.

195^v, and 196^r) contains one two-part canon at the fifth below with a non-canonic lower part;[69] and a set of 20 pieces consisting of three- to five-verse settings use faburdens derived from various plainsongs (fols. 158^r–178^v), among which the second verses of five pieces are two-part canons with one free part.[70] A 20-part canon by Bevin is found on fol. 136^r. This rather staid piece revolves around a triad on G with occasional passing notes.[71]

The most exhaustive treatment of two-part canonic imitation ever produced is George Waterhouse's 1,163 canons on the *Miserere* plainsong. Little is known about Waterhouse except that he was from Lincoln, was sworn in as a Gentleman of the Chapel Royal in 1588, and supplicated for the B.Mus. degree at the University of Oxford in 1592.[72] Morley was acquainted with Waterhouse and recommended his pupil Philomathes to study this collection:

> Yet hath one manne, my friend and fellow M. *George Waterhouse*, vpon the same plainsong of *Miserere*, for varietie surpassed all who euer laboured in that kinde of studie. For he hath already made a thousand waies (yea and though I should talke of halfe as manie more, I should not be farre wide of the truth) euerie one different and seuerall from another. But because I doe hope verie shortlie that the same shall bee published for the benefite of the worlde, and his owne perpetuall glorie, I will cease to speake anie more of them, but onlie to admonish you, that vvho so will be excellent, must both spend much time in practice, and looke ouer the doings of other men.[73]

In the sole surviving copy of the manuscript[74] the canons are organized in groups but not with consecutive numbering (fol. 1 commences with canon 1153). The plainsong is notated at the top of each page starting on either the G a fourth or an eleventh below middle C. In each case, the solution for the second canonic part is placed immediately following the leading part. Waterhouse employed canonic

---

[69]   Transcribed in Hugh M. Miller, '"Pretty Wayes: For young Beginners to Looke on"', *Musical Quarterly*, 33 (1947), 543–56. According to Miller, the term 'wayes' denotes a contrapuntal piece in two or three parts over a cantus firmus, and it appears frequently in sixteenth- and early seventeenth-century manuscripts of English keyboard music.

[70]   Hugh M. Miller, 'Seventeenth-Century English Faburden Compositions for Keyboard', *Musical Quarterly*, 26 (1940), 50–64.

[71]   This piece is transcribed in Hooper, *Bevin*, plate 11b.

[72]   Susi Jeans and John Morehen, 'Waterhouse, George', *Grove Music Online*, ed. L. Macy. <http://www.grovemusic.com>, accessed 7 February 2005.

[73]   Morley, *Introduction*, 115. The canons were never published. In the peroration, p. 183, Morley again refers to the excellence of Waterhouse's canons.

[74]   Cambridge University Library Dd.iv.60. A more detailed discussion of Waterhouse's canons may be found in Denis Collins, '"Sufficient to quench the thirst of the most insaciate scholler whatsoeuer": George Waterhouse's 1,163 Canons on the Plainsong *Miserere*', in Katelijne Schiltz and Bonnie J. Blackburn (eds), *Canons and Canonic Techniques, 14th–16th Centuries: Theory, Practice, and Reception History. Proceedings of the International Conference, Leuven, 4–6 October 2005*, Analysis in Context. Leuven Studies in Musicology, 1 (Leuven and Dudley, Mass.: Peeters, 2007), pp. 407–20.

imitation at intervals from unison to more than two octaves, the latter distances
not otherwise encountered in contemporary sources on canon. Variety in time
distances between the canonic parts likewise contributes to the great numbers of
permutations. Waterhouse makes an effort to create reasonably interesting and
varied melodic and rhythmic lines, although, unsurprisingly, awkward part-writing
is occasionally evident. Large numbers of augmentation canons, contrary motion
canons and canons employing both of these devices form the other principal
groups in the manuscript. Another smaller group explores proportional exercises
such as three semibreves against two, three against one or four minims against
three. Within the groups it is common to find second canonic parts proceeding
according to a rhythmic restrictions such as semibreves or minims only, alternating
minims and semibreves (see Example 8), or repeating ostinato-like patterns. Very
many of these procedures are found in Bevin's treatise, although with far fewer
examples to demonstrate them.

Three manuscripts contain canons that appear to be mostly by Bevin and
John Bull, with miscellaneous canons by other composers. The smallest collection
is found in British Library RM 24.f.25, an eighteenth-century collection of 24
canons, many written out in geometrical shapes, of which 18 are assigned to Bull.
Of the remainder, four are attributed to G. V. Messaus, one to Clemens non Papa
and one is anonymous. Italian or Latin rubrics accompany most of the canons in
RM 24.f.25 (*e.g.*, 'Due partes in una' or 'John Bull Doct. Fecit'), with occasional
comments in English such as 'Done' or 'Error in the plainsong' (for a missing
note in canon 4). In many cases a canon is notated as a single staff turned around
to form a circle. A staff may be enclosed within another circular staff containing
the plainsong, a non-canonic part or another leading part (in the case of a double
canon). Other canons are shaped like triangles and others are written out as
wavy lines. The last seven canons are notated with the plainsong at the top of
the page followed by the leading part in ordinary staff notation without any of
the shapes used earlier in the manuscript. French annotations accompany some
of these canons (*e.g.*, 'A la mesme Ton une mesure apres'), indicating a possible
French provenance of the manuscript for part of its history.

Six canons from RM 24.f.25, all written as puzzles in geometric shapes, appear
with full solutions in score in a set of 126 canons on *Miserere* in Österreichische
Nationalbibliothek Mus. Hs. 17.771 (hereafter ÖNB 17.771). In the second of
these manuscripts the canons follow a group of keyboard pieces in German
tablature, and all works in this source are attributed to Bull.[75] The canons are all
written in score, except for the first one, which is notated as a circle followed by
the solution written out in score.[76] The layout of voices in most of the pieces –
plainsong on top, leading part second, canonic voices next and free parts at the
bottom – shows no regard for the ordering of parts according to range. The parts

---

[75]   John Henry Van der Meer, 'The Keyboard Works in the Vienna Bull Manuscript',
Tijdschrift voor Muziekwetenschap, 43 (1959), 72–105.

[76]   This piece also appears in circular form as the fifth canon in RM 24.f.25.

Example 8   Waterhouse, canon 864, Cambridge University Library Dd.iv.60, fol. 122^r

fit conveniently across the verso of a folio continuing to the recto of the next folio so that most canons can be perused without page turns.[77] Some inconsistency results from the placement of numbers from 1 to 130 by the copyist on the recto of each folio even though there are cases where a canon occupies several pages. Bull's canons appear to have been well known to seventeenth-century musicians, with one of them (from RM 24.f.25) appearing in a book of pieces transcribed by Henry Purcell.[78]

---

[77]   The same layout is found in British Library RM 24.c.14.

[78]   Thurston Dart, 'Purcell and Bull', *Musical Times*, 104/1439 (1963), 30–31. In the last paragraph of this short article Dart refers to his forthcoming book on Bull with a detailed discussion of the *Miserere* canons. Unfortunately, this book was never published.

Most of the canons in ÖNB 17.771 are for three, four or five parts with a smaller number for six or seven parts. Typically, two or three parts engage in canonic imitation over the plainsong and a non-canonic part is present in many pieces. The manuscript itself is in poor condition with the final pages particularly difficult to read. The canons are not arranged in any particular order, although the three-part pieces (plainsong and two canonic parts) are mostly clustered between fols. 40 and 52. The *Miserere* melody appears in almost all of the canons, the exceptions being two four-part parallel canons and two augmentation canons at the end of the volume.[79] This collection employs all manner of devices: two-part imitation at intervals from unison to twelfth, three- and four-part stacked, parallel, duplex and invertible canons, use of augmentation, contrary motion and retrograde motion (sometimes in combination), and proportion exercises written in black note heads.

The manuscript ÖNB 17.771 also contains over 50 canons that appear among a set of 300 canons in British Library RM 24.c.14. However, the latter source begins with 'This Booke is written & composed by Elway Bevin'. The handwriting for these words does not resemble extant samples by Bevin,[80] and it is possible that this attribution was added by someone else. Dates are given in two places: on fol. 41^v 'July 11, 1611', and on fol. 87^r 'Aug. 10' (possibly of the same year), which fit comfortably within both Bevin's and Bull's working lives. This collection uses various plainsongs, mostly the *Miserere* melody and Morley's plainsong (from the section on canon in that theorist's treatise). Some items in RM 24.c.14 have Latin text underlay, much of which is patchy and not applied consistently to all parts. Most of the texts appear to be drawn from the Psalms. In several instances the same canons but with no texts appear in ÖNB 17.771.

There is no reason to challenge the attributions to Bull in ÖNB 17.771 and British Library RM 24.f.15, whereas the attribution to Bevin of the entire contents of British Library 24.c.14 is misleading because dozens of pieces in this source are found in the other two sources assigned to Bull. However, numerous pieces in RM 24.c.14 are very likely by Bevin, including several that appear in his 1631 treatise. It is possible that Bevin copied canons by Bull and others for his own study and included them among his own works without listing authorship for any of them. It is also possible that nothing in the manuscript is by Bevin and that he used some of the material as his own in his treatise, although this scenario is not in keeping with the comments and remarks in the treatise that indicate a pious personality.[81] It is difficult to determine clearly how the manuscript and the

---

[79]   The two parallel canons appear on fols. 121^v–122^r and fols. 132^v–133^r. Both also appear in RM 24.c.14, and the first is also in RM 24.f.25. (One other canon in ÖNB 17.771, a duplex canon on fols. 104^v–105^r, appears in the two other manuscripts.) The augmentation exercises without plainsong are items 124 and 126 in ÖNB 17.771.

[80]   Two facsimiles of Bevin's signature are in Hooper, *Bevin*, 4.

[81]   It is also possible that Bevin never owned the manuscript and the attribution to him on the first page is inaccurate.

contents of Bevin's treatise relate chronologically, except that the date July 11, 1611 suggests that Bevin may have written many of the examples over a long period and drew on some of them for the treatise. With some canons common to both RM 24.c.14 and ÖNB 17.771 there are differences ranging from a note or two at a cadence point to a more thorough reworking of the material, suggesting that Bevin was honing his skills by attempting modifications to Bull's solutions.[82] All canonic subtypes are represented by the canons found in both sources, although the largest number of pieces in both collections involve four parts: the plainsong, two canonic parts and a fourth non-canonic part.

Settings of the *Miserere* plainsong comprise the majority of the canons in RM 24.c.14 (fols. 1–87). The plainsong is placed mostly in the top register, and in all but one case is notated beginning on either the G above or below middle C (the sole exception begins on middle C). The manuscript is loosely arranged by grouping canons together according to how many parts are present, and the canons in each group are numbered. Thus, fols. 1ᵛ–15ʳ comprises 52 canons for three parts (plainsong and two canonic parts); fols. 16ᵛ–41ʳ are for four voices (plainsong, two canonic parts, one free part); fols. 41ᵛ–51ʳ have an unnumbered group of 22 pieces for five parts; fols. 51ᵛ–81ʳ have 53 pieces for five parts; fols. 87ᵛ–97ʳ contain a dozen canons for three parts followed by nine five-part pieces, all based on a new plainsong.[83] The remainder of the manuscript has some pieces based on different plainsongs, followed on fols. 104ᵛ to the end by about 50 short pieces based on Morley's plainsong. Between these groups are miscellaneous pieces and even within the groups there are occasional departures from the plainsong; for example, fols. 38ᵛ–39ʳ has 'A catch vpon ut re my fa sol la' for three parts over a plainsong-like ascending and descending natural hexachord proceeding in breves. On fols. 81ᵛ–84ʳ there are two canons notated as circles with four short melodies forming a partial square around each. One of these is attributed to Giovanni Maria Nanino and the second has the initials EB, suggesting that it was Bevin's creative response to Nanino's puzzle. Bevin provides the resolutions for both canons. Throughout RM 24.c.14 there are many instances of additional canons squeezed into available space in the margins or between the numbered canons. These pieces are not written out in score, are not included in the numbering, and are often partly illegible.

The plainsong used in the group on fols. 87ᵛ–97ᵛ was used also in canonic settings attributed to Bull in British Library RM 24.f.25 for some of the canons notated as circles, triangles and other geometric shapes. One of the canons in RM 24.c.14 (fols. 97ᵛ–98ʳ) not found in RM 24.f.25 employs a very similar triangular layout, namely, the plainsong is notated on staves arranged in a V-shape placed inside another V-shape containing notes from which a four-part canon is derived from reading the notes on each staff from left to right or right to left and starting

---

[82] For example, a two-part canon at the sixth above after a minim on fols. 47ᵛ–48ʳ of ÖNB 17.771 is modified in RM 24.c.14 fols. 2ᵛ–3ʳ.

[83] Two canons appear on unnumbered leaves after fol. 93ʳ.

either from the top left- or top right-hand side of the shape. Bevin provides the solution in score (see Figure 2), and it is possible that he wrote this canon with Bull's pieces of a similar nature in mind.

The strong connection between Bull and RM 24.c.14 is further evident on fols. 93ᵛ–94ʳ, where there is a double canon by contrary motion attributed to Bull in both British Library RM 24.f.25 and the Sweelinck theory manuscripts.[84] Bevin's version alters Bull's by small changes in rhythm and by inserting notes in places where Bull had rests, and in several places Bevin placed new notes alongside crossed-out notes from Bull's version. This supports the possibility that Bevin had access to Bull's canons and copied out many of them for his own study. Like several other canons in this section of RM 24.c.14, the plainsong is presented twice, leading to a canon that is twice as long as the one by Bull. The second half of Bevin's canon offers little difference from the first half in terms of melodic or rhythmic contour. The two versions of this canon are a further indication of the possibly quite wide circulation of plainsong canons among late sixteenth- and seventeenth-century musicians.

Several canons from RM 24.c.14 appear in Bevin's *A Briefe and Short Instruction.* On fols. 32ᵛ–33ʳ there is a set of 12 canons on the same material at different intervals of imitation and time distances[85] that appears on pp. 47–8 of the treatise. The most elaborate puzzle canon penned by Bevin involving a 63-part solution is located on fols. 79ᵛ–80ʳ of the manuscript and on pp. 45–6 of the treatise. Another piece almost identical in layout to this puzzle, except that it is based on Morley's plainsong, is found on fol. 42ᵛ of the manuscript. In the final group of pieces in the manuscript, based on Morley's plainsong, there are two canons (on fol. 108ʳ⁻ᵛ) that also appear on p. 34 of the treatise. More overlap may have been expected between these two sources, notwithstanding the fertility of Bevin's canonic talent.

Accomplished treatment of motifs and fluency in handling varied contrapuntal textures in many examples suggests that at least some of these canons may have been in Bevin's mind when, on the last page of *A Briefe and Short Instruction*, he hoped '*hereafter to set out a larger Volume, if it please God to giue me life, and enable me thereunto*'. Example 9 from fol. 1, based on Morley's plainsong, demonstrates a two-part unison canon based on a seven-note motif presented four times in succession in the canonic voices followed by two slightly modified statements.[86] The starting pitches are chosen both to outline a triad on G and to maintain consonant intervals with the plainsong. In this regard, the statement beginning on B in bar 4 forms a sixth (D–B) between the plainsong and the leading voice

---

[84]   Jan Pieterszoon Sweelinck, *Werken*, 10, ed. H. Gehrmann (Leipzig: Breitkopf & Härtel, 1901), 84.
[85]   This group may be considered collectively as a polymorphous canon, *i.e.*, when numerous solutions are possible for one piece.
[86]   The other two canons on this page have the same openings but different continuations from the second example on p. 28 of the treatise and the first example on p. 29.

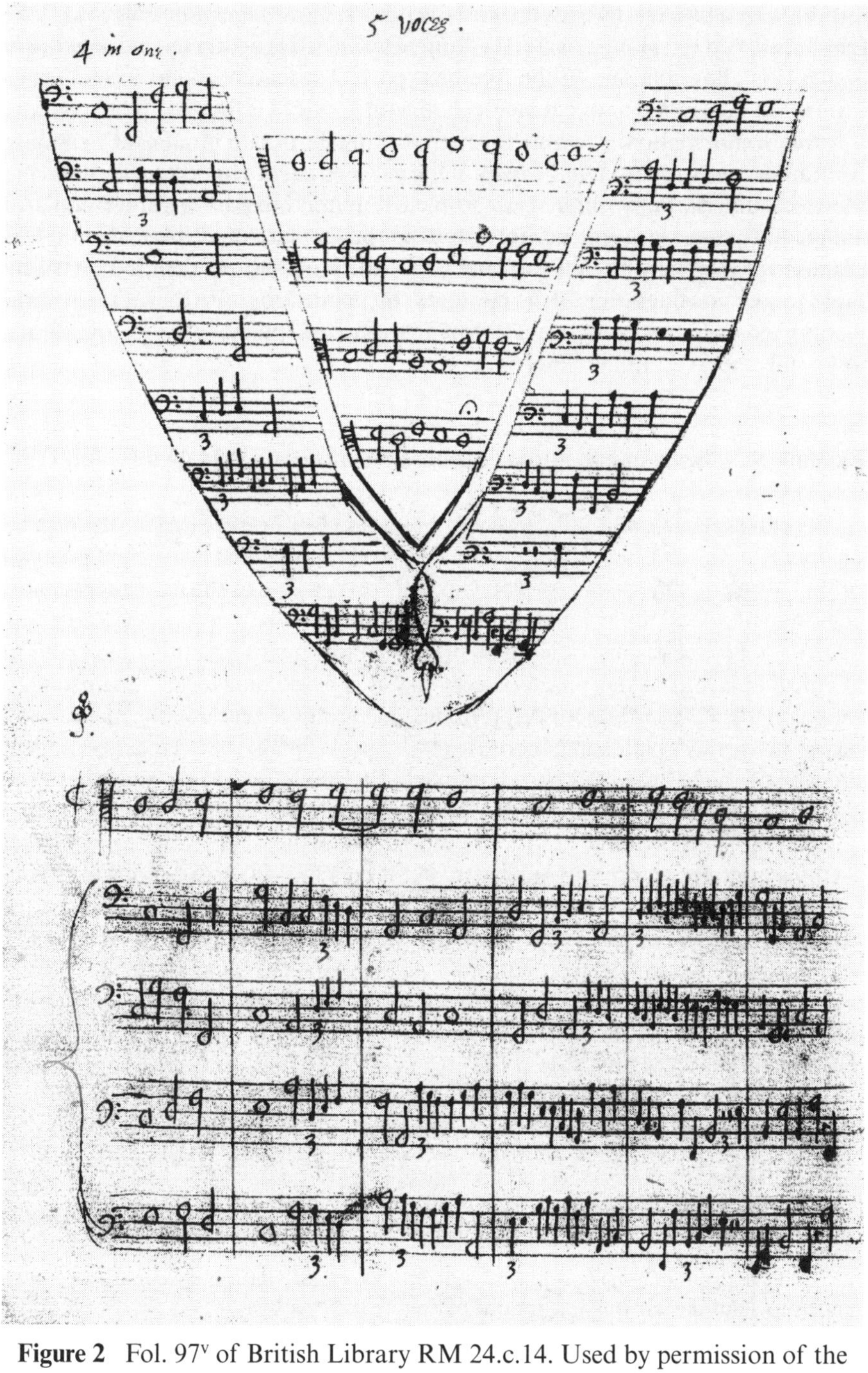

Figure 2 Fol. 97ᵛ of British Library RM 24.c.14. Used by permission of the British Library

answered by a fifth (E–B) between and the plainsong and the imitating voice. The fourth between the plainsong and canonic voices (A–D) on the second semibreve of bar 2 is allowable due to the free bass part D, a feature found in numerous canons (and discussed above in connection with Morley's examples). The bass part is woven skilfully into the texture through sharing the dotted motif and providing continuous motion through the rests in the canonic parts. However, the canons in this collection are not without their problems – numerous part-writing errors and many instances of crossed-out notes and smudgy replacements indicate that this manuscript may have been a working copy which its author intended revisiting prior to any consideration of its contents for publication. Furthermore, several pieces exist as note-against-note settings, perhaps as 'plaine' versions of canons to be fully worked out at a later time.

Example 9   Bevin canon at the unison, British Library RM 24.c.14, fol. 1ʳ

All canonic subtypes – regular motion, invertible, stacked, parallel, retrograde, contrary motion, augmentation, diminution, double canons, duplex canons and rounds – are represented in this manuscript and in the two manuscripts attributed to Bull. Generally, in RM 24.c.14 each group of numbered canons works through the intervals of imitation from unison to octave and their compound intervals. The opening pieces in a group are usually straightforward imitation canons, which are followed by pieces employing more complex devices, sometimes in combination. Many of these procedures are also encountered in Bevin's treatise and in other sixteenth- and seventeenth-century sources, although in a collection of this type it is not surprising to also encounter unusual or uniquely worked out canons. Fols. 59ᵛ–60ʳ contain stacked canons at the seventh above and ninth below (also found in ÖNB 17.771, fols. 117–118), and fols. 50ᵛ–51ʳ have a stacked canon at the sixth above. These are the only instances of stacked canons at these intervals of which I am aware. Examples of duplex canons, a term unique to this source, appear in various places, such as at fols. 72ᵛ–73ʳ, where there are two pieces with this label. Duplex canons can work in paired imitation or with equal time distances separating the voice entries, as demonstrated by Examples 10 and 11 respectively (the openings of six-part pieces with four in canon and a free bass part).[87] Some of the augmentation canons involve one of the imitating parts (usually the last part in a three- or four-part canonic texture) taking all of the notes of the leading part as semibreves only.

Example 10   Duplex canon with paired imitation. RM 24.c.14, fols. 72ᵛ–73ʳ

---

[87]   The example by Bull in both RM 24.f.25 and the Sweelinck theory manuscripts, discussed above, is an instance of a duplex canon using paired imitation. Further examples of duplex canons by Bull are in ÖNB 17.771.

Example 11   Duplex canon with equally spaced entries. RM 24.c.14, fols. 72ᵛ–73ʳ

Example 12   Retrograde inversion canon. RM 24.c.14, fols. 36ᵛ–37ʳ

Example 13   Augmentation canon at the octave. RM 24.c.14, fols. 30ᵛ–31ʳ

Bevin (or his source) is particularly adept at combining contrary motion imitation of the leading part with retrograde imitation or retrograde inversion in another part, with the latter demonstrated by Example 12. Pre-compositional restrictions such as ostinato figures derived from the plainsong or use of only certain rhythmic note values (*e.g.*, minim and semibreve alternation) in the canonic parts are explored in several pieces. Frequently found in Waterhouse's collection, the latter procedure was also popular in seventeenth-century Italian canon collections by Francesco Soriano and Giovanni Pietro Del Buono and is described by the theorist Angelo Berardi.[88] Two ingenious examples on fols. 12ᵛ–13ʳ recall *stimmtausch* (voice exchange) in that the canonic voices swap material in the second half, thereby repeating exactly what was heard in the first half. This is particularly challenging because the notes of the plainsong are different in the second half. Similar contrapuntal dexterity occurs on fols. 30ᵛ–31ʳ in an augmentation canon where the leading part is presented twice against a full statement of its augmented melody in the following part (see Example 13; the plainsong is extended by a bar).

The Contents of *A Briefe and Short Instruction*

The clear pedagogical purpose of the treatise is reflected in how its content is structured, as well as in the choice of plainsongs and presentation of examples from simple to complex. The sequence of material follows the order given in the title: discant, proportions, composing for three, four and five parts, and composing 'all sorts of canons' on a plainsong. The last of these topics is treated most extensively, and its scope goes far beyond anything found on canon in other English theoretical writings.

The first seven pages of *A Briefe and Short Instruction* deal with four rudimentary matters: consonance and dissonance, proportions, rhythmic patterns and treatment of a motif. A concise listing of perfect and imperfect consonances and dissonances on sig. A4ᵛ appears to have been widely known in the seventeenth century, judging by its reappearances (unacknowledged) in the 1664 and 1683 editions of Playford's treatise.[89] The material on pp. 1–6 deals with setting one part (a 'discant') over a short plainsong according to proportions, that is, from one to nine notes placed against the plainsong.

The first examples (pp. 1–2) start with a note-against-note setting and work up to eight notes against each semibreve in the plainsong. Next come more complex settings, starting with nine crotchets against each plainsong semibreve in the last example on p. 2. The first and second examples on p. 3 are marked 'sesquialtera' and 'sesquitertia', indicating three semibreves in the added part against two plainsong semibreves and four semibreves against three plainsong semibreves respectively. These examples use archaic notational features of ligatures and filled-in diamond-shaped note heads. Two further examples combine three-against-one ratios with nine against one or nine against two. Bevin acknowledges

---

[88]   Francesco Soriano, *Canoni et oblighi di cento et dieci sorte sopra l'Ave maris stella* (Rome: G. B. Robletti, 1610); Giovanni Pietro Del Buono, *Canoni, oblighi et sonate in varie maniere sopra l'Ave Maris stella* (Palermo: Martarello & d'Angelo, 1641); Angelo Berardi, *Documenti armonici* (Bologna: G. Monti, 1687; repr. Bologna: Forni, 1970).

[89]   Herissone, *Music Theory in Seventeenth-Century England*, 278–9.

the old-fashioned nature of these types of proportions in his comment at the end of p. 3.[90]

Each of the first four examples on p. 4 of the treatise demonstrates short repeating rhythmic motifs. Thus, the first and second examples are restricted to alternating semibreves and minims and alternating minims and crotchets respectively, which give rise to syncopation. These types of patterns are plentiful in Waterhouse's collection and also in several early seventeenth-century Italian compendia of counterpoint.[91] The following two examples on p. 4, 'Driuing an odde Mynome to the end' and 'Driuing an odde Crochet to the end', involve placing a minim or crotchet rest at the beginning, which leads to syncopated patterns. The last two examples on this page, 'Subdupla' and 'Subtripla', are the only instances where the plainsong moves in faster note values than the added part. The final topic considered in the opening pages is the 'manner of maintaining a point'. The examples on p. 5 show how a short rhythmic motif can be used three or four times starting on the same or different pitches. The examples on p. 6 demonstrate the same procedure for two imitative parts over a plainsong; the last example on this page involves contrary motion ('The point reuerted').

Bevin turns to 'two partes in one' on p. 7, thus beginning his treatment of canon, the topic that occupies the remainder of the treatise. Unlike discussions of contrapuntal techniques by other writers, Bevin offers no explanations for terminology, notation, or devices such as contrary motion or retrograde motion, and no rules or guidelines for composing any kind of canon. He makes occasional remarks about the difficulty of canonic writing and identifies some canons according to procedures such as *'per arsin et thesin'*, *'recte et retro'*, 'double discant' or augmentation. Bathe and Morley focus on two-part canonic imitation, though Morley (and later Simpson) do refer in passing to more complex canonic forms such as retrograde canons (*recte & retro*), stacked canons or canons *per tonos*. In contrast, Bevin presents a large number of examples of diverse canonic types; it is perhaps this feature that prompted Purcell's high praise at the end of the century. All of the canonic techniques in Bevin's treatise may be found in the manuscript collections discussed above. Examples of complex canonic procedures are rarely present in the compositional repertoire of the period, and their cultivation was principally in the domain of personal collections not destined for publication.

---

[90] Many canons employing proportional exercises can be found in the manuscript collections of Waterhouse, Bull and Bevin. Pieces of this type are also found in English repertoire of the period, for example in British Library RM 24.d.2 (the Baldwin Commonplace Book); see *British Library RM 24.d.2*, introduction by Jessie Ann Owens, Renaissance Music in Facsimile, 8 (New York, 1987).

[91] See Michael Lamla, *Kanonkünste im barocken Italien, insbesondere in Rom* (Ph.D. diss., University of Saarbrücken, 2003).

The presentation of canons in Bevin's treatise moves systematically from two-part imitation canons in regular motion to multi-voice examples demonstrating different procedures and structures. A small number of puzzle canons is located towards the end of the treatise. Bevin provides fully written-out solutions for almost all of the canons; for some of the later examples he gives only the beginning of each part in the solution (*i.e.*, the canons *per tonos* on pp. 33 and 36, a canon for 63 parts on pp. 45–6 and polymorphous canons on pp. 47–50). Otherwise, his directions and solutions are easy to follow. In two cases (pp. 44, 46), he employs both red and black inks, and the solutions to these puzzle canons require that different parts be assigned notes according to colour. The types of canons and numbers of voices involved may be summarized as follows:

Plainsong 1

7–15	3 parts	Imitation in regular motion from unison to octave above at increasing time distances.
16		Repeated motifs in non-imitative examples.
17–23	3 parts	Augmentation, retrograde, contrary motion, invertible counterpoint.
24–7	4, 5 parts	Double canons. Three in one.

Plainsong 2

28–31	4 parts	Regular, contrary motion and invertible counterpoint for two canonic parts and one free part.
32–44	4, 5 parts	Double canons in regular and contrary motion. Derivation of plainsong in semibreves. Canons *per tonos*, stacked, duplex canons.

Plainsong 3

45–52	up to 63 parts	Puzzle canons, polymorphous canons

Three plainsongs are used in the treatise: pages 1–27[92] use a short seven-note melody in stepwise motion, the only exceptions being two examples on p. 16. Pages 28–44 use the melody that Morley used in his discussion of canon. Pages 45 to the end use the *Miserere* melody much favoured by English composers. Bevin does not consider cases where there is no plainsong; neither does he comment on

---

[92] Throughout this discussion references will be made to the original page numbers in the treatise. These are indicated by square brackets in the edition.

whether the canonic melody may have any relationship to the melodic contour of the plainsong (in most examples it does not). The order of plainsong melodies reflects a pedagogical ordering from beginner's material to intermediate level to a plainsong suitable for an accomplished contrapuntist. Of the seven notes comprising the first plainsong used in the treatise, the first five are the same as the opening of the *Miserere* melody and last two notes were probably added by Bevin to bring about a cadence on D. Bevin is clearly aiming the first 27 pages at a beginner, and the examples of two-part canons on pp. 7–16 arranged systematically at intervals of imitation from unison to octave and at gradually increasing temporal distances support this orientation. The number of parts increases to four at p. 24 in order to show how the plainsong may be treated canonically.

The canons based on Morley's plainsong demonstrate contrary motion, retrograde motion, augmentation and invertible counterpoint. Examples of double canons, stacked canons, duplex canons, rounds and canons *per tonos* provide a thorough survey of canonic counterpoint. The increased variety in rhythmic and melodic details among these canons reflects the pedagogical structuring of material from introductory to contrapuntally accomplished examples.

The canons on *Miserere* reflect the most complex and individual approaches to contrapuntal ingenuity and craftsmanship. The *Miserere* melody was a logical choice for this given the history of its settings in English music. It was the vehicle for the most virtuosic displays of canonic writing by Bull, Waterhouse, Woodson and the pseudo-Byrd, most of which was probably known by Bevin (as the incorporation of Bull's *Miserere* canons in British Library RM 24.c.14 may indicate). It is therefore a logical and fitting conclusion to the treatise to demonstrate some particularly erudite canonic artifice on the *Miserere* plainsong.

Two-part canons in regular motion at different intervals of imitation and time distances are dealt with on pp. 7–15 of the treatise.[93] The plainsong is placed in the top and middle register in the two canons on p. 7; thereafter it is almost always placed in the lowest register. These canons are arranged according to the temporal distance between the canonic parts, starting with a crotchet and moving systematically through minim and semibreve, with a series of canons from unison to seventh or octave above (but none at intervals below) for each of these distances. On p. 15 there is an example at a distance of three minims and another example at a breve distance.

As Bevin provides no guidance on how to write canons, it is useful to keep in mind the method of writing canons in plain and divided versions that informs the canonic theories of Bathe and Morley (and later Simpson). This provides a useful tool for considering how Bevin maintained consonant canonic structures. As Morley and Bathe make clear, the melodic intervals of the leading part and the harmonic intervals formed between that part and the plainsong are

---

[93]   The list of intervals from unison to seventh given on p. 7 of the treatise presumably assumes compound interval equivalence.

calculated at the time distance of the canon – the 'plaine' version. The 'diuided' version fills out the texture through varied rhythms, and passing, repeated and returning notes.

In the first canon on p. 8, at the unison after a crotchet, the leading part must form a consonant harmonic interval on the last crotchet of the plainsong semibreve that will lead to a consonant interval between the second canonic part and the onset of the next plainsong note.[94] For plainsong progressions descending by step, Bevin has a fifth between the plainsong and leading part at this point, which becomes a sixth between the next plainsong note and the following part. In fact, this is the only intervallic combination that maintains consonance among all parts when the plainsong descends by step in a unison canon, and it is the only possibility corresponding to this situation listed by Bathe in his tabular method for composing canons. Bevin turns this restriction to advantage by creating a sequential pattern in those bars where the plainsong descends by step. This example has several features in common with Morley's divided versions of canons: frequent parallel motion in thirds between the canonic parts, varying the leading part through use of passing notes and by repeating notes either at the same pitch or at the octave. Many of the examples on pp. 7–15 show how the plainsong acts as corrective to fourths between the two upper canonic parts, a feature also noted in the discussion of Morley's canons (see Examples 1a and 1b above).

Four of the six progressions in the first plainsong are descending seconds. Scrutiny of the succession of these intervals in bars 3–6 of the regular motion canons on pp. 7–15 reveals that Bevin very often favours the same harmonic intervals between the plainsong and leading part at those points affecting the harmonic intervals of the subsequent plainsong-following part. For instance, in the canon at the third above after a crotchet (p. 8, last example), tenths are formed between the plainsong and leading part on the last crotchet for each descending plainsong semibreve in bars 3–6. These become consonant thirteenths between the plainsong and second canonic part. In canons at the unison or sixth there is no choice because only one harmonic interval between leading part and plainsong will preserve consonance between the plainsong and second canonic part (a fifth becomes a sixth in the former, a sixth becomes a twelfth in the latter). Yet even in canons where more choices are available, Bevin mostly pursues the same harmonic

---

[94] In a canon at a crotchet distance, the harmonic interval formed between the leading part and the last crotchet of each plainsong semibreve requires careful attention because the following part will imitate the leading part at the onset of the next plainsong note. Likewise, in a canon at a minim distance, the note in the leading part at the onset of the second minim of the plainsong semibreve will be imitated by the following part when the plainsong moves to its next note; similarly, in canons after a semibreve the plainsong-leading part harmonic interval at the onset of each plainsong semibreve will affect the plainsong-following part harmonic interval at the onset of the next plainsong note.

intervallic relationship between leading part and plainsong in bars 3–6. This often leads to sequential or quasi-sequential patterns in the melodic contours, as in the filled-in descending fifths in the canon at the fourth above (p. 9, first example) or the dotted minims and quavers in the canon at the sixth above (p. 9, third example). Other examples, however, vary the choice of intervals between the parts, as in the canons at the seventh above (p. 10, first example; p. 15, first example), although this does not lead to noticeably different melodic or rhythmic profiles in the canonic parts.

Two points may be noted about the canon at the unison after a breve (p. 15, third example). First, this is the only member of the group of canons in regular motion that so far contains a fourth free part, the bass (which covers the eleventh between the plainsong and leading part at the beginning of bar 3). Second, because of the temporal distance of this canon, the harmonic intervals between plainsong and leading part affect the harmonic interval between plainsong and second canonic part two bars later. Therefore, a descending third occurs between bars 3 and 5 and between bars 4 and 6, and this is taken into account in Bevin's choice of harmonic intervals between the plainsong and leading part.

On p. 16 there are two examples 'maintaining their seuerall points' and using Morley's plainsong. These non-imitative pieces recall the examples on pp. 5–6 and show how individual motifs can be repeated in the upper parts, a challenging task as each motif must work against the changing plainsong notes.[95] These examples also recall Morley's use of repeated motifs in Examples 3 and 4 above.

Pages 17–23 introduce augmentation, contrary motion (*per arsin & thesin*), retrograde motion (*recte & retro*), and invertible counterpoint ('Double discant'[96]). Like other theorists, Bevin considers retrograde canons the easiest of all to compose, although it is 'somewhat difficult to be made vpon a Plainsong'. He introduces double discant on p. 20 with almost the same words as Morley used when introducing this subject.[97] In Bevin's first example the imitation is not strictly maintained, whereas the next example, on p. 21, is a 'double discant in a Canon'. These examples are given in two forms, called 'Principall' and 'Reply', and both employ invertible counterpoint at the twelfth. The last example on p. 21 uses ¢ and reverse ¢ to demonstrate imitation by diminution and contrary motion (See Figure 3, p. 88). Similar use of these notational signs can be found in the

---

[95]   Because they contain three parts, Bevin may have placed these two examples on p. 16 rather than with the other examples on Morley's plainsong (pp. 28–44), which have four or five parts.

[96]   Bevan uses the spelling 'discant' whereas 'descant' is otherwise found in English sources.

[97]   Morley: 'though it be no Canon, yet is it verie neere the nature of a Canon' (*Introduction*, 105). Bevin: 'is no Canon, but somewhat of the nature of a Canon' (*Instruction*, 20).

manuscript collections of Waterhouse, Bull and Bevin, although it is infrequent in canonic repertoire examples from the period.

The two examples on p. 22 and the first on p. 23 combine contrary and retrograde motion in note-against-note examples based on the plainsong melody.[98] In the second example on p. 23, the notes of the plainsong are derived by imitating the notes of the leading part as semibreves in contrary motion. The plainsong in the third example on this page is found by taking alternating notes of the following part as semibreves. Further examples in which the plainsong is derived from the canonic parts are explored in canons based on Morley's plainsong (discussed below).

A series of four-part pieces commence on p. 24 of the treatise. In the double canons ('foure in two') on pp. 24–5, one pair of voices manipulates the plainsong by means of contrary motion, retrograde motion or retrograde inversion, while the second canon is in regular motion based on unrelated melodic material. Starting with the second example on p. 25 and continuing through p. 27 there is an exploration of three-part canonic writing in augmentation and double augmentation, sometimes in combination with contrary or retrograde motion. The latter two procedures are found together in the second example on p. 27, the only five-part piece based on the first plainsong.

Bevin introduces the second plainsong (from Morley's treatise) without comment on p. 28. Examples are in four parts until p. 37 and then in five parts until p. 44. While many types of canonic writing are demonstrated in this section of the treatise, from p. 32 onwards the examples of each type are not grouped together; rather, the examples move from one procedure to another with occasional placement of two or more pieces of the same type together. Double canons are presented in four- and five-part examples and demonstrate various procedures in their constituent two-part canons.

The examples on pp. 28–31 comprise two imitative parts, the plainsong and a free part (often marked 'Ad placitum'). The material of the free part is often related to the two canonic parts, which proceed in regular or contrary motion. Included in this group is a 'Double discant made in a Canon' on p. 30 for which Bevin gives the 'reply' in invertible counterpoint at the octave. In this piece Bevin appears to be responding to the challenging remarks made by Morley about the great difficulty of writing a contrary motion canon upon a pre-existent plainsong.[99]

---

[98]   These examples bring to mind the first canonic section of Purcell's 'Fantazia: three parts on a ground' where there is a canon 're[c]te et retro & arsin per thesin'. Henry Purcell, *Fantazias and Miscellaneous Instrumental Music*, rev. edn, ed. Michael Tilmouth, Alan Browning and Peter Holman, The Works of Henry Purcell, 31 (London: Novello, 1990), 53. The note-against-note setting and the short length of Purcell's piece recalls the examples on pp. 22–3 of Bevin's treatise.

[99]   Morley, *Introduction*, 114–15. On p. 114 Morley also says that canons *per arsin & thesin* 'carie both most difficultie, and most maiestie', words that are echoed by Bevin when

Two double canons on p. 32 demonstrate how the plainsong can participate in the canonic writing. In the first example, the plainsong is derived by taking only the crotchets from the top part (*i.e.*, the first leading part) and augmenting them to semibreves. The second example includes one pair of voices in canon at the second above on the plainsong melody. In the following four-part examples, the plainsong and the fourth part are integrated in various ways with the canonic writing. To underline this point, Bevin introduces the next pieces as 'certaine Canons of diuerse and sundry sorts, which are many of them very difficult to be made to any Plainsong', a point repeated several times in the following pages.

In the second example on p. 34, the two upper parts form a unison canon after a breve while the plainsong is derived by taking only the minim notes of the leading part and placing them at the fifth below as semibreves. Similarly, the first example on p. 35 has a canon at the octave in the two upper parts, while the tenor arrives at the plainsong by imitating the leading part in contrary motion in semibreves only. In the first example on p. 37, another double canon, the plainsong is derived in semibreves only from the first four bars of the free bass part. Among the five-part examples, the lowest part of the first canon on p. 39 imitates the part above in semibreves only to obtain the plainsong. A similar approach, not involving the plainsong, is evident in the first example on p. 34, where the second following part imitates the leading part in contrary motion in semibreves only.

Two canons 'after the manner of a Round' appear on p. 33, one 'falling a note at euery returne' and the next 'riseth a note at euery returne'. These are examples of canons *per tonos* where the transposed repeated material is not provided by Bevin. In these canons, the music repeats through the whole tone scale until the opening pitch is reached again, up or down an octave. The unimaginative melodic lines in the two canonic parts are adorned by rhythmically more active free parts. Another canon *per tonos* appears on p. 36 to the text 'O Iesus dulcis remissio omnium peccatorum meorum' (O Jesus, sweet forgiveness of all of my sins). The melodic profile of the three canonic parts is more assured in this example.

Two examples of three-part stacked canons on the plainsong appear as the second piece on p. 35 and the first on p. 36. The former is at the second above and the latter is at the fifth above. The subtlety of canon *per tonos* procedure at the second above is also incorporated into the example on p. 36. Bevin provides part of the second statement of the music, showing how it will proceed through a circle of fifths starting on C and modulating to G for the second statement that will likewise move to D, and so on through remaining keys, thus establishing a clear tonal orientation for the piece. Compositions incorporating technical difficulties to this extent are not numerous in the English repertoire, although Bevin's contemporary, Thomas Tomkins, wrote a three-part stacked canon at the

---

introducing contrary motion canons on p. 18 of his treatise: 'both difficult, and carrieth more maiesty than any other Canon'.

fifth below combined with canon *per tonos* at the second below in the first half of his Fantasia 10.[100] In the eighteenth century two canons of this type were used by Rameau to engage with the theories of Zarlino, and Kirnberger also wrote two such canons that are remarkable for their blend of contrapuntal virtuosity and chromatic harmonies.[101]

Of the 14 five-part examples on pp. 37–44, eight are double canons mostly involving regular-motion imitation at the unison. Paired imitation is demonstrated in the two double canons on p. 40, while the second example on p. 42 is a double canon involving one pair of voices in regular motion and the other in contrary motion.

Duplex canons appear on pp. 38 and 41. Unlike many examples in the manuscript collections, these pieces involve imitation at the fifth (first example p. 38) or twelfth (second example p. 41). The examples on pp. 38 and 41 involve three canonic parts and a free fifth part. A closely related piece, not involving contrary motion, is the second example on p. 38, where the first following part imitates at the fifth below and the second following part is at the unison with the leading part.

The most unusual procedure from this section of the treatise occurs as the first examples on pp. 41 and 43 involving 'either part repeating that the other sung before'. This is related to the duplex canon because the second part is in contrary motion and the third part, if present, is in regular motion. However, the leading part is constructed so that its second phrase is a contrary-motion version of the first phrase and is, in fact, identical to the opening phrase of the following part. The melodic material of the leading part comprises a number of segments lasting two or three semibreves that are separated from each other by rests. The canonic voices alternate these segments so that a type of voice exchange occurs.

The example on p. 41 is a double canon in which the upper two parts are engaged in alternating segments (contrary-motion versions of each other) while the lower two parts have a unison canon in regular motion. On p. 43, the upper three parts each comprise four segments presented in the same order by the first and third parts but with the middle part taking them in contrary motion, leading to a patchwork of alternating motifs. Also in this example, the plainsong departs from its regular semibreve presentation from bar 4 onwards through use of faster rhythmic figurations. The lowest part begins by imitating the plainsong before continuing in free writing. These two examples are constructed very similarly to Byrd's contrary motion canon quoted by Morley (see Example 5

---

[100] Thomas Tomkins, *Consort Music*, ed. John Irving, Musica Britannica, 59 (London: Stainer and Bell, 1991), 27–9.

[101] Alan Gosman, 'Rameau and Zarlino: Polemics in the *Traité de l'harmonie*', *Music Theory Spectrum*, 22 (2000), 44–59. Denis Collins, 'Bach's Occasional Canon *BWV* 1073 and "Stacked" Canonic Procedure in the Eighteenth Century', *BACH*, 23/2 (2002), 15–34.

above). They may indicate Bevin's familiarity with this canon and his creative responses to it.

The last example to use Morley's plainsong is a puzzle involving red and black note colours on p. 44. The solution, provided by Bevin, involves one part taking all of the notes, another taking red-coloured notes only, and a third part taking black notes only.

The final part of the treatise, pp. 45–52, comprises six canons on the *Miserere* plainsong which contrast greatly with the material so far. Two of these canons involve multiple solutions, one incorporates a duplex canon with an ostinato, and the three others involve solutions for 6, 21 and 63 parts. Based on the longest of the three plainsongs used in the treatise, these canons demonstrate Bevin's abilities in the area of puzzle canons.

The first of these canons, on pp. 45–6, a quadruple canon whose solution requires 60 canonic parts, is just such a demonstration, even though the resulting texture with its constantly repeating motifs does not achieve much musical merit. Two free parts are notated below the plainsong, leading to a 63-part composition in total. The plainsong melody is interrupted in bars 12 and 13 by a four-note figure with a rest on either side that is in red notation in the original printed edition. The six parts placed above the plainsong are derived according to the Latin instructions placed above and below these notes. 'Diapente superior 15' means that this red-note figure is transposed up a fifth and 14 voices imitate it (giving a total of 15 parts in this canon). In the example this figure is placed in the part second from the top and the first imitating voice is written on the staff underneath. Another 13 parts would likewise imitate at the unison after a breve. The two parts notated immediately above the plainsong correspond to the first two voices of the fifteen-part canon derived according to the text 'Tertio inferior *per Arsin & Thesin* 15' ('third below by contrary motion 15'). The monotones E and D in the topmost part and the part fourth from the top correspond to the other two Latin instructions and each requires fifteen parts in the solution. One begins each bar with a rest because 'Retro' is included in the instructions. According to Bevin, these 'two are halfe Canons, because they take onely the later parts, which is the Semibriefe and Semibriefe Rest'. The challenge in writing this canon appears to have been in discovering a repeating motif that would work against all of the plainsong notes. The erudition of the piece is supported by the Latin poem on p. 46, which recalls the canonic inscriptions accompanying many medieval and Renaissance puzzle canons.

The example on pp. 47–8 is a polymorphous canon with twelve solutions. This is a demonstration of considerable contrapuntal acuity in finding twelve solutions over the same plainsong. Bevin provides the full written-out version on p. 47 for the version at the unison, and on the following page he only gives the opening notes for the other 11 pieces. All but one of the 12 versions are two-part canons with a third free part, and the exception is a stacked canon at the fifth above (the fifth version, marked 'Diapente superior' on p. 48). As noted above in the discussion of plainsong canon collections, this canon and the 63-part canon both appear in British Library RM 24.c.14.

A canon with four solutions based on invertible counterpoint for four parts (quadruple counterpoint) is presented on pp. 49–50. The first reply is derived according to invertible counterpoint at the octave, while invertible counterpoint at the twelfth is used in the second and third replies. Bevin's text lists the alterations for the three replies according to each voice. All of the examples are in regular motion and thus correspond to Zarlino's and Morley's first category of invertible counterpoint (the second category involves contrary motion). Another nuance in the example is that the plainsong travels downwards through the voices from the highest (treble) in the 'principall' to the bass in the final reply.

A 21-part example on p. 51 comprises four five-part unison canons over the plainsong. This quadruple canon has unusually widely spaced barlines after every five semibreves to reflect the temporal distance between the voice entries. This undertaking may have been in part a response to one of Giovanni Maria Nanino's 20-part canons written out by Bevin in RM 24.c.14. The following pages of the manuscript contain a similar canon with Bevin's initials. The resulting texture of the 21-part canon in the treatise shows remarkable control over melodic and rhythmic balance between the parts, indicating perhaps that Bevin's study and reflections upon Nanino's example were fruitful.[102]

The last page of the treatise contains two canons. The first is texted in both parts and the top part is a version of the plainsong modified by repeated notes in order to accommodate the text. The lower part is the leading part of a five-part unison canon at a distance of five semibreves, a distance that is again reflected in the barring of Bevin's example.

The last example is based on three-part canonic imitation of an ostinato motif accompanied by an independent bass part and a modestly decorated version of the plainsong. The ostinato is treated as a duplex canon with contrary motion and regular-motion imitation at the octave below. The accompanying rhyming verse refers obscurely to 'Fifteene parts in one', which may simply mean that the five notes of the ostinato sung by three parts equals fifteen parts derived from the single notated line. The reference to Christ in this verse is one of many religious allusions during the course of the treatise, including the Latin text in the previous canon. So many references of this nature may in part have aroused the suspicions of Bevin's contemporaries, including his employers at Bristol Cathedral, although the exact circumstances of Bevin's declining fortunes in his later years cannot be determined. The concluding comment that the material presented is 'sufficient for young Practitioners at this present', again highlights the pedagogical intention of the treatise, notwithstanding the complex nature of many examples, in particular those towards the end of the text. Bevin's legacy in this treatise is an exposition of the art of canon in a systematic arrangement suitable for students of this discipline, with a thorough presentation of procedures

---

[102] A transcription written out by hand is in Hooper, *Bevin*, plate 16b.

and techniques that occupied the attention of many musicians in sixteenth- and seventeenth-century England.

English Theories of Canon after Bevin

English theorists from the mid and late seventeenth century who consider canon are Charles Butler, Christopher Simpson, John Playford and Henry Purcell (in his revision of Playford's treatise). Of these writers, Christopher Simpson provides the most comprehensive introduction to writing canons for the beginning student, and his discussion will be considered at length below. Butler deals mainly with definitions of terms for imitative counterpoint almost entirely derived from Morley and the *Melopoeia* of Seth Calvisius,[103] the latter of which is based on the chapters on imitative counterpoint in Zarlino's *Le istitutioni harmoniche*. Butler's advice to the reader to study and imitate the 'best Autors' is most likely a commonplace sentiment shared by theorists, especially those, like Bevin and Purcell, who provide an extensive number of examples often demonstrating complex canonic techniques but without commentary on their construction.

The fourth edition (1664) of Playford's treatise reproduces the table of concords and discords from the preface to Bevin's treatise, while the tenth edition (1683) additionally gives several canons from pages 10 to 14 of Bevin's work.[104] Playford does not acknowledge his source. In the 1694 revision of the twelfth edition, Henry Purcell refers the reader to 'a wonderful variety of *Canons* in Mr. *Elway Bevin's* Book ... where you will meet with all the Variety of *Canons* that are to be made'.[105] Purcell divides imitative counterpoint into eight categories of 'Fuge', of which canon is 'the eighth and noblest sort'. Purcell's discussion of tonal answers has been commented on as a noteworthy contribution to fugal theory,[106] but his presentation of numerous examples for each of the eight categories is unaccompanied by explanatory text. He gives his own examples of two-, three- and four-part canons and a four-part example by Blow, but his accompanying text is limited to the praise of Bevin's book (quoted above).

Bevin's name appears in eighteenth-century sources, beginning with a mention in the commonplace book of Johann Sigismund Cousser (or Kusser,

---

[103] Charles Butler, *The Principles of Musik* (London: John Haviland, 1636), pp. 73–7. Seth Calvisius, *Melopoeia sive melodiae condendae ratio, quam vulgo musicam poeticam vocant* (Erfurt, 1592).

[104] John Playford, *A Brief Introduction to the Skill of Musick*, 4 edn (London: William Godbid for John Playford, 1664), before p. 1, and Playford, 'A Brief Introduction to the Art of Descant' in *An Introduction to the Skill of Musick*, 10th edn (London: William Godbid for John Playford, 1683), 2, 26–7, 29.

[105] John Playford, *An Introduction to the Skill of Musick*, 12 edn revised by Henry Purcell, 1694, sigs. I2, I7 (pp. 169, 175). Reprint ed. with Introduction by Franklin B. Zimmermann (New York: Da Capo Press, 1972).

[106] Playford, *Introduction,* rev. Purcell, ed. Zimmerman, 30.

1660–1727).[107] There was very little consideration of canon by eighteenth-century English theorists; those who mention it just give brief definitions and sometimes advice for writing a two-part canon derived from Simpson's treatise.[108] Brief biographies of Bevin are given by both Hawkins and Burney, who praise his treatise as being useful to students on the grounds that canons at that time were 'regarded as the greatest efforts of human intellect' (Burney), and that Bevin 'generously communicated the result of many years study and experience in a treatise which is highly commended by all who have occasion to speak of it' (Hawkins).[109] At the end of the century, A. F. C. Kollmann included five puzzle canons by Bevin in the section on imitative counterpoint in his *An Essay on Practical Musical Composition.*[110]

Among English theoretical sources from the sixteenth to eighteenth centuries, Simpson's *Compendium* provides the most useful instruction for the beginning student of canon. He devoted the fifth of the five parts of his *Compendium* to 'The Contrivance of Canon' and noted at the outset that 'Divers of our Countreymen have been excellent in this kind of Musick; but none (that I meet with) have publish'd any Instructions for making a Canon.'[111] This remark recalls Morley's comment about the lack of general rules for writing canons, and it would seem that Simpson was unaware of Bathe's method for writing canons. He continues by stating that 'Mr. *Elway Bevin* professes fair, in the Title page of his Book; and gives us many Examples of excellent and intricate Canons of divers sorts; but not

---

[107] Beinecke Rare Book and Manuscript Library, Yale University, Osborn Music Ms. 16: 'Mr Elway Bevin's Boock, published 1631, has wonderfull variety of Canons'. Cousser probably began the book after he arrived in London in December, 1704, and the list of items in which Bevin's book is included was almost certainly made after he settled in Ireland in 1707. I am grateful to Samantha Owens for bringing these details to my attention.

[108] Johann Christopher Pepusch, *A Treatise on Harmony*, 2nd edn (London: W. Pearson, 1731; repr. Monuments of Music and Music Literature, second series, vol. 28. New York: Broude Bros, 1966); Giorgio Antoniotto, *L'arte armonica; or a Treatise on the Composition of Music* (London: J. Johnson, 1760); William Tansur, *The Elements of Musick Display'd* (London: Stanley Crowder, 1772).

[109] Hawkins, *A General History of the Science and Practice of Music*, 505. Burney, *A General History of Music*, 263–4.

[110] Augustus Frederic Christopher Kollmann, *An Essay on Practical Musical Composition* (London: the author, 1799; ed. Imogene Horsley, New York: Da Capo Press, 1973), 57, 72–3. All of the examples in this treatise are grouped together in a series of plates, with Bevin's canons appearing on plates 40–41. In its structure and choice of examples from the seventeenth and eighteenth centuries, with an emphasis on Bach, this part of Kollmann's treatise appears to be modelled on Friedrich Wilhelm Marpurg's *Abhandlung von der Fuge* (Berlin: Haude & Spener, 1753–4).

[111] Christopher Simpson, *A Compendium of Practical Musick*, 3rd edn (London: H. Brome, 1678 [1st edn 1665; 2nd edn 1667]), 147. All references and transcriptions are from the third edition.

one word of Instruction how to make such like'.[112] The perceived lack of existing instructional material for writing canons probably prompted Simpson to provide guidelines for the student 'because the exercise thereof will much enable you in all other kinds of Composition; especially where any thing of Fuge is concerned, of which, it is the principal'.[113]

Simpson's focus is on showing the beginning student how to write regular-motion canons at the unison. He begins with a step-by-step approach for two parts and expands the discussion to include voice-leading patterns for three-part examples over a ground or plainsong, some of which are given in plain and divided form. There are also several short sections on different types of canonic writing, but these comprise little more than a series of examples.

To write a two-part canon at the unison, the student devises notes for the first bar of the leading part, copies these in the following part one bar later, then finds suitable notes for the leading part in bar 2, and in such manner continues to the end of the piece. This process can be applied generally to two-part canons regardless of the interval of imitation, the time distance chosen or the starting voice. Simpson notes that if the student should 'perceive that your following Parts begin to run counter one upon another' then new notes should be found or a rest inserted.[114]

In a three-part canon at the unison, Simpson notes that 'each Part doth begin in the same Tone, it necessarily follows, that the foregoing Parts must move into the Concords of the said Tone'.[115] The example he provides (Example 14), is an arpeggiation of the tones concordant with 'the said Tone'.[116] This and the following example recall Morley's plain and divided versions of examples. They show how the canonic voices are structured around triadic arpeggio notes that can be filled in with passing notes and varied with different rhythmic values and changes of melodic direction including octave leaps. In addition, Example 15 demonstrates how the intervals of fifths and sixths can be exploited to provide changes and contrast in harmony, and how the canon may be broken at a cadence point.

The next section, '*Of Syncopated or Driving Canon*', deals with canonic entries at a crotchet time distance, which 'may be applied to any Ground or Plain-song consisting of *Semibreves*; or of *Breves*'.[117] A set of guidelines is provided for constructing three-part canons according to the interval by which

---

[112] Ibid., 147. This statement has been interpreted by Rebecca Herissone and Barry Cooper as a criticism of Bevin, although it may be just a plain statement of fact without any intended criticism. See Herissone, *Music Theory in Seventeenth-Century England*, 202; Cooper, 'Englische Musiktheorie im 17. und 18. Jahrhundert', 165.

[113] Simpson, *Compendium*, 147.

[114] Simpson, *Compendium*, 153.

[115] Ibid., 154.

[116] Ibid., 155.

[117] Simpson, *Compendium*, 156.

Example 14   Simpson, Concords for a tone. *Compendium*, 155

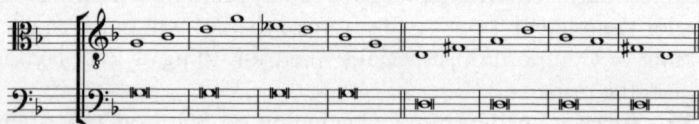

Example 15   Simpson, canon at the unison. *Compendium*, 155

the ground or plainsong moves. Unlike Bathe's material on canon, which also deals with permitted intervals according to how the plainsong moves, Simpson's presentation is a model of clarity suitable for students, although it is restricted to just one case – a canon at the unison after a crotchet with the ground as lowest part. When the ground ascends by step (in semibreves) the leading part should form harmonic intervals of a third on the first minim and a sixth and a fifth on the remaining notes, as demonstrated in Example 16. When the ground descends by step, a pattern of a third followed by a fourth and fifth is employed. In other cases where the ground ascends or descends by fourth or fifth, the leading part forms a third with the onset of each note of the ground (larger intervals in the ground are not considered). These precepts are combined in a three-part example at the unison (Example 17),[118] which is followed by the same example 'in Plain Notes, that you may better perceive, both the Syncopation, and also how the Parts move' (Example 18).

Example 16   Simpson, patterns for stepwise ground. *Compendium*, 156

Bevin's examples at the unison after a crotchet do not adhere to Simpson's recommended patterns except for using a fifth in the leading part on the last crotchet of a descending plainsong semibreve (the only interval that will lead to a consonance between the plainsong and leading part on the next plainsong semibreve). This is demonstrated in the first example on p. 8 of *A Briefe and Short Instruction*. The second example on p. 29 places the plainsong in the top part; other canons at a crotchet distance are at different intervals of imitation.

Two invertible canons by Matthew Locke conclude this section on the driving canon, both without a ground (see Examples 19 and 20).[119] Simpson simply states that the parts 'proceed from 3*d.* to 3*d.* … And break off to a 4*th.* the contrary way, to keep the Canon in due *decorum*; which otherwise, would ascend or descend beyond due limits.' This results in a sequential progression, similar in contour to the previous examples. Example 20 is a contrary-motion version of Example

---

[118]   In the original, the E flat in the key signature of the top part is omitted. It is included in Example 9.

[119]   Ibid., 161–2.

Example 17   Simpson, '*Canon in Unison to a Ground*'. *Compendium*, 158

Example 18   Simpson, The same canon 'in plain Notes'. *Compendium*, 159

19 using invertible counterpoint at the twelfth (with a half-bar extension at the end), unremarked by Simpson.[120]

Example 19   Simpson, invertible canon by Matthew Locke. *Compendium*, 161

Example 20   Simpson, same canon inverted at the twelfth. *Compendium*, 162

The remainder of Simpson's treatment of canons comprises several short sections on different canonic subtypes. Although he gives examples in all cases, his accompanying text mostly does little more than go beyond saying that writing them 'depends upon sight; and therefore no Rule to be given; excepting the helps formerly mentioned'. This comment occurs in Section 6, '*Of Canon a Note Higher or Lower*', where there are two examples, again by Matthew Locke, of stacked canons at the second above and below.[121] Likewise, section 7, '*Of Canon Rising or Falling a Note*' has two canons *per tonos* without any detailed commentary.[122]

The next section deals with retrograde canon ('*recte & retro*'), which 'may seem a great Mysterie, and a business of much Intricacy, before one know the

---

[120] It is tempting to think that Locke wrote these short canons expressly as demonstrations suited to Simpson's section on canon, except that a longer version of the first of these examples is found as a setting of the Sanctus from the Mass Ordinary in the manuscript British Library Add. 30933, fol. 129ᵛ.

[121] Simpson, *Compendium*, 163. The Lord edition, based on the 1667 edition, includes a sentence missing from the 1678 edition in which Simpson acknowledges Locke's assistance with the treatise.

[122] Ibid., 165.

way of doing it: but that being known, it is the easiest of all sorts of Canons.'[123] Simpson's explanation of the retrograde procedure is the same as given by all theorists who deal with this topic, namely, that one starts with a short two-part piece and then continues the top line with the retrograde of the lower part and likewise continues the lower part with the retrograde of the top part.[124]

Simpson describes another type of canon *recte & retro* in which a four-part piece comprising two trebles and two basses can be reworked as a two-part treble and bass piece – in essence the reverse procedure of what he has just described. The two upper voices become one longer voice when one of them is attached in reverse to the other; likewise with the two lower parts. Simpson goes on to say that the four-part texture can be retained when each part continues with the retrograde of its companion part, and that similar pieces for six and eight parts can work in this manner. This recalls Morley's eight-part canon *recte & retro* at the end of the third part of his treatise. The only rule Simpson gives is that care should be taken with dotted notes, which will fall on the wrong side of the notes in the retrograde version, and with discords which may occur at the beginning rather than the second half of a note. Apparently he means that care should be taken with suspensions because the dissonance and consonance will be in the wrong order in the retrograde version. Simpson commits this very error in his own four-part example where the first treble has a 4–3 suspension in bar 4. This creates an awkward dissonance if the piece is continued in retrograde. In Example 21, the first four bars are from Simpson's text while bars 5–8 are a continuation applying retrograde motion according to his guidelines. The continuation is overall consonant except for bar 5 in the second treble, where the retrograde of the suspension formula in bar 4 leads to an incorrectly resolved dissonance (C) in the second part from the top.

The only reference to contrary-motion imitation (*per arsin & thesin*) in Simpson's treatise occurs in the context of a very short section on invertible counterpoint ('Double Descant'). A rule that double descant at the octave should avoid using fifths because they become fourths in the inversion is accompanied by an example that also employs contrary-motion imitation.[125] The result is a musical curiosity.

The next section, 'Of Canon to a Plainsong proposed', returns to canonic writing in the presence of a long-note pre-existing melody.[126] Simpson states this 'which I am now to speak of, cannot be reduced to any Rule (that I know,) as depending merely upon sight'. He takes a canon by Bevin (the second example from p. 14 of *A Briefe and Short Instruction*) and shows how it is constructed. This is nothing more than the bar-by-bar approach where the student needs to find notes for the leading part 'as may agree, both with the present Note of the

---

[123] *Compendium,* 166–9.

[124] Nicola Vicentino was the first theorist to describe retrograde writing in his *L'antica musica,* ch. 37.

[125] Simpson, *Compendium,* 169–71.

[126] Ibid., 171–74.

Example 21 Simpson, four-part retrograde canon. *Compendium*, 167

Plainsong, and serve the following Part for the next Note of the Plainsong also'. This method works at any distance of imitation and with the plainsong above or between the other parts according to Simpson. Two further examples (not by Bevin) are added at the end of this section without further discussion.

The final section of Simpson's treatise deals with '*Of Catch or Round*'.[127] This is constructed by devising a four-bar piece for four equal voices and then having one voice sing all four parts with the other voices entering after a time interval of four bars. This is the same method as given by Morley and is a procedure for writing canons found in several Continental treatises beginning with Burmeister's *Musica poetica* (1606) and appearing in the writings of Kircher, Marpurg, Albrechtsberger and Kollmann.[128] It is a clear and concise approach to writing simple unison or octave canons and was probably generally known amongst musicians in general.

In summary, Simpson's treatment of canon is primarily concerned with guiding the beginning student through canonic imitation in regular motion for two or three parts. In contrast with earlier English sources for canon, the *Compendium* is less concerned with plainsong canonic settings or with more specialized procedures such as contrary motion, retrograde motion or augmentation. It provides a pedagogical perspective quite distinct from the exposition of diverse kinds of canonic writing offered in Bevin's treatise.

---

[127] Simpson, *Compendium*, 174–5.
[128] Collins, 'Canon in Music Theory', 138–43.

PART II

Elway Bevin,
A Briefe and Short Instruction of the Art of Musicke

Editorial Note

The edition retains most features of the original text, including original capitalization, spelling, punctuation and font (italic or roman). Page numbers are given in square brackets. Placement of the text and examples in the edition corresponds as closely as possible to the original locations in the printed treatise, but there are difficulties at times in interpretation. We must remember that the printer was in effect translating Bevin's manuscript original, and he does not seem to have maintained uniform procedures with regard to choice of font size, typeface and spacing. This is evident in the main text, containing information and comments about different topics as well as explanations of procedures in musical examples. In addition, the headings and labels for musical examples are often difficult to differentiate. This edition employs consistency in font size, spacing and indentation, and it distinguishes headings from labels by placing the former above the musical examples and the latter where they occur in the original, that is, above or between staves. The footnotes to the edition comment on unusual text placement in the original.

The musical examples in the original are printed in open score with page breaks interrupting some examples. The edition retains open score and changes the page breaks where appropriate. Original note values are retained, as are the barlines. Double barlines are not present at the end of examples in the original but are supplied in the edition. The final measure in Bevin's examples typically ends with a semibreve and sometimes even a minim, above which is found a fermata. Examples with bars of unusual length are commented upon in the endnotes. Bevin rarely gives time signatures, but almost all of the examples have one or two plainsong semibreves per bar. The treble and bass clefs are retained in the edition but the C clefs are replaced with treble, transposed treble (down an octave) and bass clefs. The original clefs are shown at the beginning of the transcribed examples. In some instances, particularly among the *Miserere* canons at the end of the treatise, Bevin provides only partial solutions. Full solutions are included in the edition for most of these, except for the canons *per tonos* on pp. 33 and 36, the canon for 63 parts on pp. 45–6 and the 21-part piece on p. 51 of the treatise because these would be very cumbersome and would add little to what can be understood from the notated versions that Bevin provides. Explanations of the canonic procedures involved in the musical examples may be found in the introduction to this edition, pp. 40–51. The footnotes to the edition comment on unusual features or errors in the examples.

Bevin's placement of accidentals is also retained, including those places where he repeats the same accidental within a bar. Sharp signs are usually found a little below the notes to which they apply, and in the edition they are placed to the left of notes. Placement of fermatas is also retained except for those occurring under notes in the original, which are placed above notes in the edition without comment. All dots acting as ties across barlines are altered to ties without comment. Beams are used to connect smaller note values, again without comment. Instances of ligatures, red ink (in examples on pp. 44 and 46) in the original are indicated by square brackets placed above the notes and commented on in the notes.

Eight surviving copies of the treatise are located in institutions in the United Kingdom and United States. Two copies are held by the British Library, shelf marks RM 15.f.2 and K2.d.14. The latter is in fragile condition but all of the text is present and readable. It serves as the base copy for the present edition. Other copies are located at the Library of Congress, Royal Academy of Music, Royal College of Music, Huntington Library and Bodleian Library (formerly held at St Michael's College, Tenbury). The copy held at Cambridge University Library is missing all pages prior to p. 1. The Royal Academy of Music copy survives in poor condition; the bottom corners of pages 7, 28, 32, 41, 51 and 52 are very worn or missing. Sig. A3 to p. 2 of the Royal College of Music copy are replaced by a copy of these pages on slightly larger paper than used in the rest of the book. The contents of sig. A4ᵛ and pp. 1–2 are also written out untidily on three pages appended to the back of this copy. Pages 1–34 of Bevin's treatise are copied, sometimes out of order, in the manuscript British Library Add. 30933 (fols. 41–59).

Copies of the original book at the Royal College of Music, Cambridge University Library and British Library K2.d.14 have no alterations to the text, whereas the other five copies contain several stop-press corrections as well as corrections in ink possibly added in-house after completion of the print run. All of these amendments are present in the Library of Congress, Huntington and British Library RM 15.f.2 copies, while the Bodleian and Royal Academy of Music copies have most of them. Stop-press alterations involve corrected clefs (pp. 8, 10), corrected notes (pp. 48, 51) and altered text underlay (p. 52). In-house alterations in ink comprise inclusion of the words 'Dr. Goodman' in the dedication, corrected notes (pp. 33, 43, 49), and addition of fermatas, ties or custodes (pp. 24, 26, 34, 52). The corrections to pp. 8, 10 and 33 are also found in British Library Add. 30933. This edition incorporates all of these changes except for those in the first example on p. 52 because the leading canonic part is not altered in any source to match the modified text underlay. All of the corrections and the copies in which they occur are listed in the footnotes to the edition. The footnotes also point out uncorrected errors in the surviving copies.

British Library K2.d.14 has numbers written in ink between the staves for the first three examples on p. 1 and the second example on p. 5. These represent the harmonic intervals formed between the parts. The Bodleian copy also has harmonic intervals written in ink above the top staff in examples on pp. 1–2 and between the staves on pp. 22, 23, and 26. These were probably added by later owners of these copies of the book. Apart from these additions, no copy of the treatise contains any further isolated alterations to the text.

[sig. A2ʳ]

A

BRIEFE AND

SHORT INSTRVCTI-

ON OF THE ART OF

Mvsicke, to teach how to
make Discant, of all proportions that are in vse:

VERY NECESSARY FOR ALL

such as are desirous to attaine to knowledge in the Art;

And may by practice, if they can sing, soone be able
to compose three, foure, and five parts: And also to compose all sorts of Canons that are usuall, by these directions
of two or three parts in one, upon the Plain-song.

By Elvvay Bevin.

[Printer's mark]

LONDON,

Printed by *R. Young*, at the signe of the *Starre* on Bread-street hill. 1631.

[sig. A3r]

TO THE RIGHT REVEREND FATHER IN GOD, AND MY HOnourable good Lord, Dʳ. Goodmanᵃ the Lord Bishop of GLOCESTER.

RIGHT REVEREND,
AFter much paines taken in the study and art of Musicke, for these many yeares last past, to compose Canons of two & three parts in one upon the Plain-song; have now at length laid downe this burden of my minde, the hopefull issue of my tyred braine. To the visiting of which Infant, many of my good friends resorting, and those skilfull in my profession, perswaded me to expose it to the world, and let try for it selfe; which I refused to doe, untill I called to minde, that it might tend to the praise and glory of Almighty God, and to the benefit of my native country: Yet finding, that such exposed Infants might easily perish without the protection of some worthy and powerfull Patron, resolved to keepe it at home, untill I remembred your good Lordship to be a lover and favourer of Musick, and unto whom I have beene much bound for many favours, for all which, being not able to returne worthy compensation, but rather to trench more and more [sig. A3ᵛ] [running head:] *The Epistle Dedicatory*
daily upon your benignity, doe bequeath this my Infant unto your Lordships Patronage, whom I know for authority, wisedome, and learning to be able, and for piety and charity will bee willing, to protect the same; which if you vouchsafe, you have and always shall have devoted

To your Lordships service,

ELVVAY BEVIN.

[sig. A4ʳ]
TO THE READER.

BEing no lesse true than ancient, that good things common are of more regard, I might not imbrest this talent (the perfection of my long endeavours) and not impart it to the publique benefit, lest I should prove my selfe no Moralist, and so incurre their blackest censure, who first did backe me on this enterprise. I doubt not the perusers favour (yet not glory in my little one) if hee vouchsafe it but a slender tryall; for though it be but small in quantity, yet for diversities of examples and

---

ᵃ   The words 'Dʳ. Goodman' are added by hand here in all extant copies of the original apart from British Library K2.d.14 and the copies at Cambridge University Library and the Royal College of Music.

difficulties, the quality may seeme the greater, and passe the elaborate workes of larger volumes. Thine,

Elway Bevin.

To Mr Elway Bevin *upon his Canons of three parts in one.*

An E P I G R A M.

MUsicke breaths heaven, nay more, it doth disclose it,
If old Iudicious *Bevin* doe compose it.
Astronomy stares high, and doth not feare
To draw heavens curtaine, and unfold a Spheare:
But Musicke climbes as high as *Iacobs* Scale,
Out-vies a *Iacobs* Staffe: it doth unvaile
Three for her one, or rather three in one:
A mystery that Art ne're thought upon.
Three parts in one, are no Trichotomy
Of one in three, but a sweet Trinity
Combin'd in one. This may (with wonder) make
An Atheist (if hee'le lay his eares to stake)
Sing Trinity in Vnity, when he shall
Heare that (which he thought harsh) prove musicall.
Church Musicke finds applause, then why not Hee
That sets forth Canons of a Trinity?[1]

Thomas Palmer.

Bristoll.

[sig. A4^v]

There are nine Concords of Musicke, as followeth:

A *Vnison, Third, Fift, Sixt, Eight, Tenth, Twelfth, Thirteenth, and Fifteenth:* Whereof five are called perfect, and foure unperfect.
    The five perfect, are, *Unison, Fift, Eight, Twelfth* and *Fifteenth:* Of these you may not take two of one sort together, neither rising nor falling, as two *Fifts* or two *Eights.*
    The other foure, called unperfect, you may take two or three together of one sort, rising or falling, which are, a *Third, Sixt, Tenth,* and *Thirteenth.*

These nine Concords are comprehended in foure, *viz.*

Unison,
Eight,   } are counted as one, for every eight is the same.
Fifteenth,

Third,
Tenth,   } likewise.

Fift,
Twelfth,   } likewise.   So that in effect there are but foure
                                               Concords.

Sixt,
Thirteenth,   } in like sort.

The Discords are, a *Second, Fourth,* and *Seventh,* with their *Eights*; which being sometime mixt with Concords, make best musicke, being orderly taken.

[1] The proportions, as follow.

Conterpoint:[b]

Dupla.

Tripla.

---

[b]   The first three examples of British Library K2.d.14 have numbers added in ink between the staves. The Bodleian copy has numbers added above the top staff in all four examples on p. 1. The numbers indicate the harmonic intervals between the parts.

Quadrupla.

[2] Quadrupla by three.

Sextupla.

Octupla.

Nonupla.

[3] Sesq. altera.

Sesq. tertia.[c]

Sesq. tertia.

Tripla Inductio to Nonupla

Sesq. altera Inductio to 9 2.

---

[c]   Square brackets placed above notes in the top part of this example indicate ligatures in the original.

Divers other proportions there are, as Quintupla,
Septupla, and such like, which are out of use.

[4] Semb. And Mynome.

Mynome and Crochet.

Driuing an odde Mynome to the end.

Driuing an odde Crochet to the end.

Subdupla.[d]

---

[d] In the original this heading occurs between the staves of the musical example, most likely for reasons of space.

Subtripla.[e]

[5] The manner of maintaining a point.

Another Example.[f]

Another of the same.

Another of Sextupla.[g]

---

  [e]   This heading also occurs between the staves of the musical example in the original.

  [f]   Numbers added between the staves in British Library K2.d.14 indicate the harmonic intervals between the parts.

  [g]   Minims in the original are notated with stemless black notes.

[6] 3. Voces.   2. partes to the plain-song:[2]

The point reuerted.

[7] *The ordinary wayes of two partes in one, are as followeth.*

2. in one
in the

$\left\{ \begin{array}{l} \text{Vnison.} \\ \text{Second.} \\ \text{Third.} \\ \text{Fourth.} \\ \text{Fift.} \\ \text{Sixt.} \\ \text{Seventh.} \end{array} \right\}$

Of these sorts you may make upon one Plain-song a thousand wayes, onely by altering the Rests, and setting the Plain-song sometime above, sometime below, and sometime in the middest, which causeth great variety, as for example you may partly see, by these that follow.

Plain-song above. A Crochet following.[h]

Plainsong in the middest.

---

[h] The fermata over the note E in this example indicates the final note to be imitated by the following part.

[8] Plainsong belowe:[3]

A Crochet following.[i]

---

[i] The plainsong C2 clef in British Library K2.d.14, Cambridge and Royal College of Music copies is replaced by a C4 clef in all other copies.

[9]

[10]

A Mynome following.^j

---

^j　In the second example at a minim distance (i.e., the third example on p. 10 of the original), the plainsong C2 clef in British Library K2.d.14, Cambridge and Royal College of Music copies is replaced by a C4 clef in all other copies.

[11]

[12]

[13] A Semibriefe following.

[14]

[15]

Three Mynomes following.

Two Semibriefes following. 4. Voces.[4]

[16] Thus may you increase your Rests, if the Plain-song be of any length, to eight or tenne *Semibriefes*, or more, before the following part cometh in. And in this order might a great number of wayes be made: But I will not counsaile any to the pursuit thereof; for I hold it better to know the way and meanes how it may be done, than to take so laborious a worke in hand.

Two parts to the Plainsong maintaining their seuerall points.^k

Another example of the same.

[17] There are diuerse other wayes of two parts in one, which are not so common, but yet more difficult in composing, as two in one *per Augmentation,* that is, when one part doubleth euery Note, making the Crochet a Mynome, the Mynome a Semibriefe, &c.

Example.⁵

___

^k   The original has a sharp before the note G at the beginning of bar 6 in the top part.

Another example.

[18] Also you haue two parts in one *per Arsin & Thesin*, by contrary motions, that when one part ascendeth the other descendeth, which is both difficult, and carrieth more maiesty than any other Canon: And are diuersly made in any distance.

Example.

Another example.

Canon *per Arsin & Thesin.*

[19] Moreouer you haue two in one Recte & Retro, when one part singeth forward and the other backward, which is somewhat difficult to be made vpon a Plainsong, but without, the easiest of all other. Many other wayes there are, and are daily inuented by the skilfull, as you shall perceiue by these examples that follow.

Canon. Recte and Retro:

Another below.

Canon. Recte and Retro.

Another.[6]

Canon. Recte and Retro.

[solution:]

[20] There is also a kinde of double discant which is no Canon, but somewhat of the nature of a Canon, and sometime also made in a Canon.

Double discant.

The Principall.

In the Reply the Treble is set eight notes lower and made the Counter, and the Base is set twelue notes higher and made the Treble, the Plainsong set an eight lower and made the Base.

The reply.[7]

[21] Double discant in a Canon.

The Principall.[1]

In the Reply the higher of the principall is set an eight lower and made the Base, and the Base set a fift higher and made the Counter, and the Plainsong being the Treble set eight notes lower.

The Reply.[8]

Diminution by turnes *per Arsin & Thesin.*[9]

[solution:]

[22] Here are certaine Canons of three in one, very difficult, made of the Plainsong it selfe; euery part contrary to other in nature.[10] These are compound Canons,

---

[1]   These words are placed between the top two staves in the original, most likely for reasons of space.

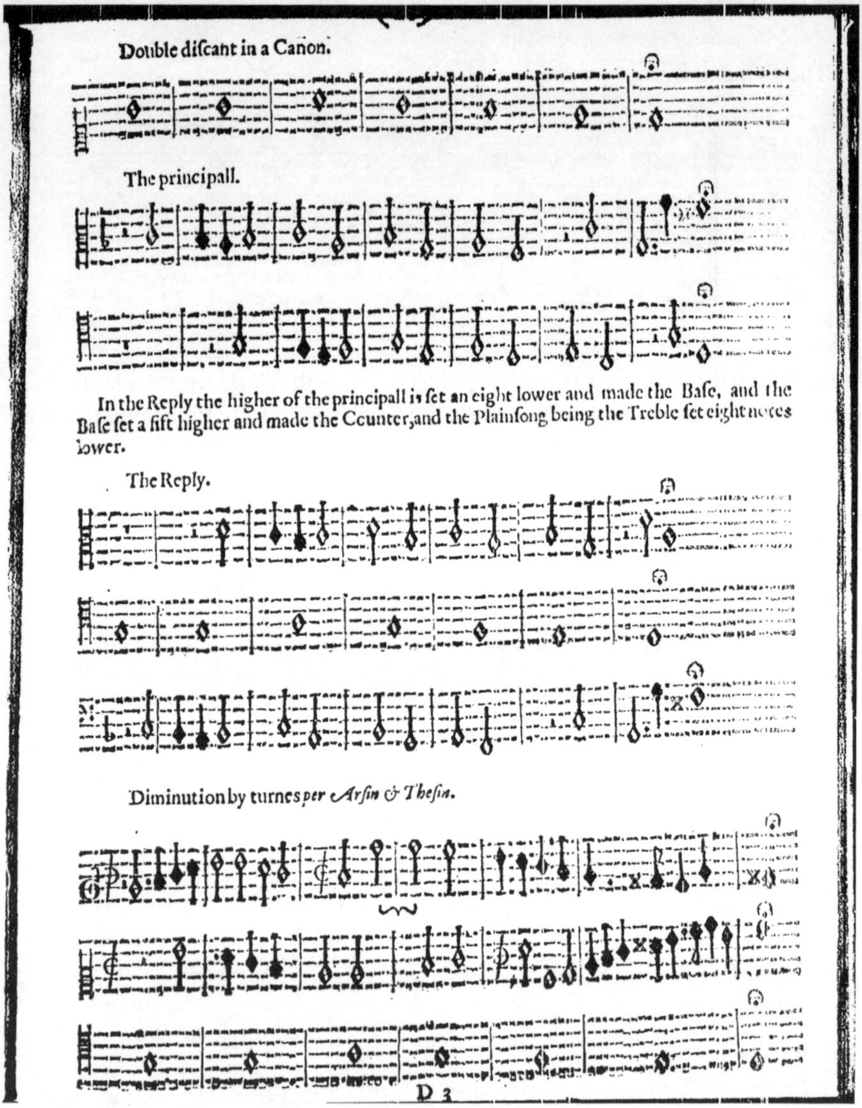

Double difcant in a Canon.

The principall.

In the Reply the higher of the principall is fet an eight lower and made the Bafe, and the Bafe fet a fift higher and made the Counter, and the Plainfong being the Treble fet eight notes lower.

The Reply.

Diminution by turnes *per Arfin & Thefis*.

D 3

Figure 3 Page 21, *A Briefe and Short Instruction of the Art of Musicke*. British Library K2.d.14. Used by permission of the British Library and ProQuest Information and Learning Company. Further reproduction is prohibited without permission.

euen as the Apothecary maketh his confections of diuers simples, compounded together of sundry wayes.^m

Another example, *per Arsin & Thesin.*[11]

I have set them downe very briefe and short, and haue made choise of this Plainsong of purpose, to the intent, the Learner or Practitioner may the better conceiue of euery particular, being also set downe in partition.

[23]

Example.

Example.

Canon three in one, *per Arsin & Thesin,* making euery note a Semibriefe

Take one and leaue one *per Aug.* So the Plainsong contained therein.[12]

Canon three in one.

[24] Foure in two. 4. Voces.

Canon.

Canon *per Arsin & Thesin.*

Another foure in two.

Canon Recte & Retro *& per Arsin & Thesin.*

Canon.

Another foure in two.[n]

[solution:]

[25] Another of foure in two.

---

[n] In all copies of the original the fermata is placed over the note E in the penultimate bar of the plainsong. The Huntington, Library of Congress, Bodleian and British Library RM 15.f.2 copies erase the custos placed to the right of the first minim G in bar 2, where it is found in all other copies, and place it above this note. They also add a custos above the second note of the plainsong. These two custodes indicate where the following parts should enter in the solution.

Per Augmentation. Aliud crescit in Duplo.[13]

These canons that follow are also very difficult to be made on any Plainsong.

[26] Three in one of sundry proportions.°

Another of like difficulty.

[27]

°   The Library of Congress, Huntington, Bodleian and British Library RM 15.f.2 copies include the tie between the last two notes in the top part. The superfluous fermata over the penultimate note in this part is present in all copies of the original. The instruction *Crescit in duplo* applies to the second part from the top.

Crescit in duplo, leauing the rest at the beginning.

Per Arsin & Thesin.

Canon three in one.

Five in two, *Recte & Retro & per Arsin & Thesin.*

Canon three in one, *Recte & Retro.*

Canon two in one, Recte & Retro.

[28]   A Mynome following.

Canon in diatessaron.

Ad placitum.

[29]   A note aboue.

Mynome and Crochet binding one vpon another.[14]

[30] Double discant[p] made in a Canon.[15]

---

[p] All copies of the original have a dot instead of a crotchet rest after the minim C in the following part (second from the top) in bar 3.

In the Reply the Meane is made the Base, set eight notes lower, the Base is made
the Meane, set eight notes higher.

[31]   A note aboue.[q]

---

[q]   In all copies of the original there is an unnecessary tie between the last two notes
in the second part from the top.

Canon in the third.

[32] This Canon singeth onely the Crochets Semibriefes, the other onely the Crochets making them Briefes.

Canon. Foure in two. 4. Voces.

Canon.

Foure in two.[r]

Here follow certaine Canons of diuerse and sundry sorts, which are many of them very difficult to be made to any Plainsong.

[33] This Canon may be sung after the manner of a Round, falling a note at euery returne, and falling note by note to the end.[s]

---

[r]   The plainsong is varied in bar 4 in order to avoid consecutive octaves with the top part, and also in bar 5 to maintain consonance with the lowest part.

[s]   In British Library K2.d.14, Royal College of Music and Cambridge copies the final two notes in the last full bar are B and C. These are erased and replaced with D and E in all other copies, thus avoiding parallel unisons with the second part from the top.

This Canon riseth a note at euery returne, and riseth note by note to the end.[t]

[34] Two parts falling, the third rising, making euery note a Semibriefe.[u]

---

[t] The plainsong is varied in bars 3 and 4 to avoid parallel octaves with the bass.
[u] A fermata is present above the high G in the second last bar in the top part in the Huntington, Bodleian, Library of Congress and British Library RM 15.f.2 copies but absent in the other copies. The fermatas in the top part indicate the last notes imitated by both following parts.

The third part singeth onely the Mynomes making them Semibriefes,[16] *per Aug.*[v]

Canon three in one Vnison.

A Canon of three in one, hath resemblance to the holy Trinity, for as they are three distinct persons and but one God, so are the other three distinct parts, comprehended in one. The leading part hath reference to the Father, the following part to the Sonne, the third to the holy Ghost.

---

[v]   A fermata is added above the D in the second last bar in the top part in the Huntington, Bodleian and Library of Congress copies. This fermata indicates the last note imitated by both following parts.

[35] Diapson. *Aliud per Arsin & Thesin* making euery note a Semibriefe.[17]

A note aboue Another.[w]

---

[w] The crotchet B in the leading part (second from the bottom) in bar 2 is given as a quaver in the original text.

[36] Rising a note at euery returne, a fift one aboue another.

Rising a note at euery returne.[x]

O Ie-su dul-cis re-mis - si-o om-ni - um pec-ca-to - rum

me - o - rum   O   Ie - su

---

[x]   In bar 5 the plainsong rhythm is varied and an extra note, C, is added in the original. Also, the last note of the plainsong is placed between the note A and the barline of bar 7 of the original. The text may be translated as 'O Jesus, sweet forgiveness of all of my sins'.

[37]   Foure parts in two.^y

Fiue voc. foure in two.

^y   The fermata sign over the A in the bass in bar 4 should be over the next note, G, which indicates the final note of the plainsong (derived in semibreves from the bass part).

[38]   Fiue Voc.[z]

Ad placitum

Canon three in one *per Arsin & Thesin & Vnison*

---

[z]   The plainsong contains an extra note, C, in bar 5.

Canon three in one.

[39]   Foure in two.

Foure in two:

[40] Foure in two.

Foure in two.

[41]   Foure in two, either part repeting [*sic*] that the other sung before.

Canon three in one *per Arsin & Thesin.*

[42] Foure in two.

Canon.

Canon.

These Canons be of different natures, therefore the more difficult.

Foure in two.

[43] This Canon is very difficult to make vpon any plainsong, either part repeating that the other sung before.[aa]

Canon three in one *per Arsin & Thesin & Vnison.*

[aa]   All copies apart from British Library K2.d.14, Cambridge and Royal College of Music correct the last note from A to C in the second part from the top.

[44] Five Voc. This Canon is to be prict in two seuerall colours.[18]

Canon three in one.

The red is one part, the blacke another, the third part singeth both colours, leauing all the Rests, as appeareth below.

The Canon explained.

Here follow certaine Canons, which are most difficult in composition, by reason of the great variety of Canons contained in them.

[45] This Canon hath a resemblance to the frame of this world, for as this world doth consist of the foure Elements, viz. Fire, Ayre, Water, and the Earth, and in either of them sundry liuing and moueable creatures: So likewise this Canon consisteth and is deuided into foure seuerall Canons, and to euery one belongeth fifteene parts, a certaine number for an vncertaine.

The whole sixty parts are contained in these seuen. These figures are set to distinguish the parts.

Here it is to be noted, that the following parts of euery Canon rest two Semibriefes after other, euery Canon different in nature.[ab]

[ab] In the original this line of text is placed between the staves of the plainsong and the part above it (the third and fourth parts from the bottom). In the original, this example is spread over two pages; the custodes after bar 7 indicate the page break.

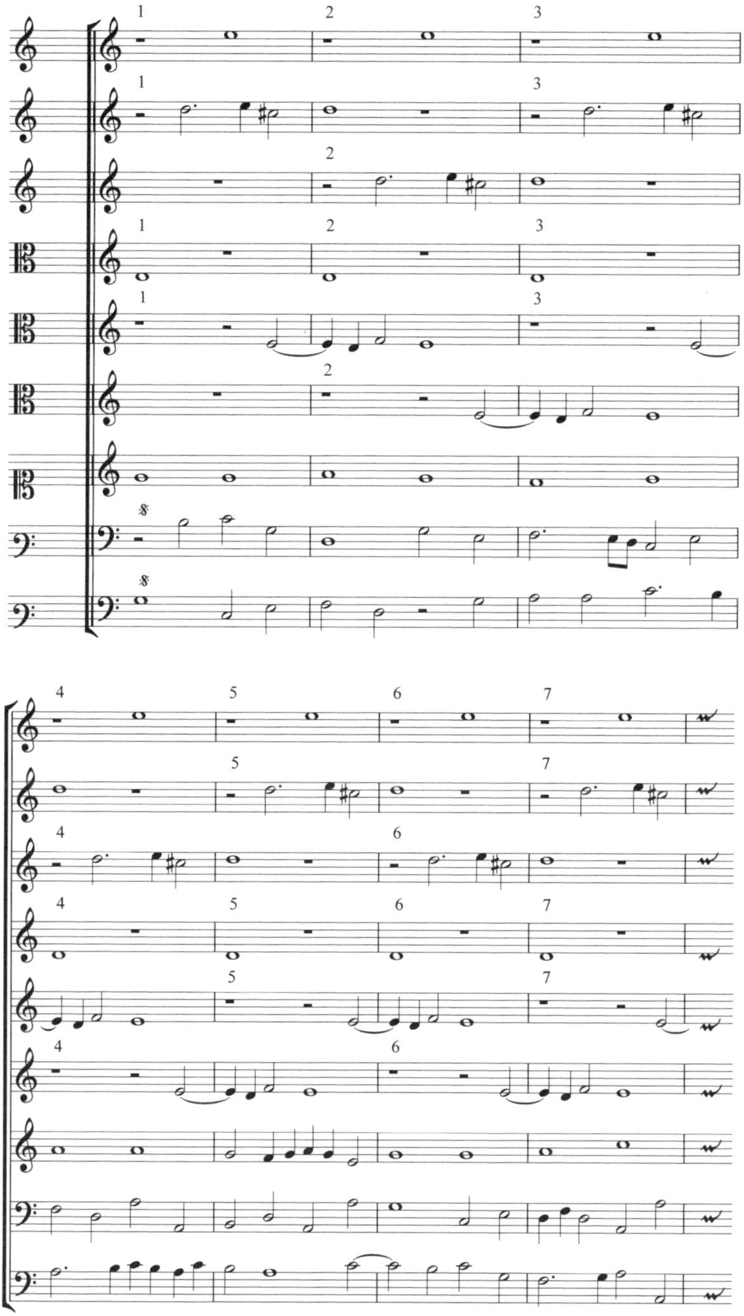

1
2
3
4
5
6
7

You shall vnderstand that in the Canon, which is the red, is diuided into foure seuerall Canons, and to euery of them belongeth fifteene parts, in the whole three score: Two of these Canons are whole, and two are halfe Canons, because they take onely the later part, which is the Semibriefe and Semibriefe Rest, and are to be sung in diuers tunes according to the direction.

[46]

Bis binos capit Canon verosque Canones:
Integri duo sunt, dimidiique duo.
Horum quisque Canon vero terquinque requirit:
At primo debent caetera cuncta Cani.
Sed iuncto duplici Basso ponitur infra,
Vocibus isto nouem singularite Canas.[19]

These threescore parts in one are contained in foure red notes.[ac]

[47] This Canon is to be sung in all distances, as appeareth in the page following.

[ac] Notes and rests in red ink in the plainsong in the original are indicated by a square bracket placed above them.

Foure Voc.

[48] He that will looke into the depth of this Canon, must take the paines to pricke out euery one of these at large, for I haue set downe only the beginning of euery part, to saue labour: And so likewise in the next that followeth.[ad]

The Plainsong neuer changeth, neither the Base, but onely in the fift way, which is the Canon set eight notes lower.

The other two parts may easily be prict according to the directions set downe already.

[ad]   The first note in the bass in version 10 is corrected from D to C in all copies except British Library K2.d.14, Cambridge and Royal College of Music. Also, the minim rest at the beginning of the bass in version 12 is an error.

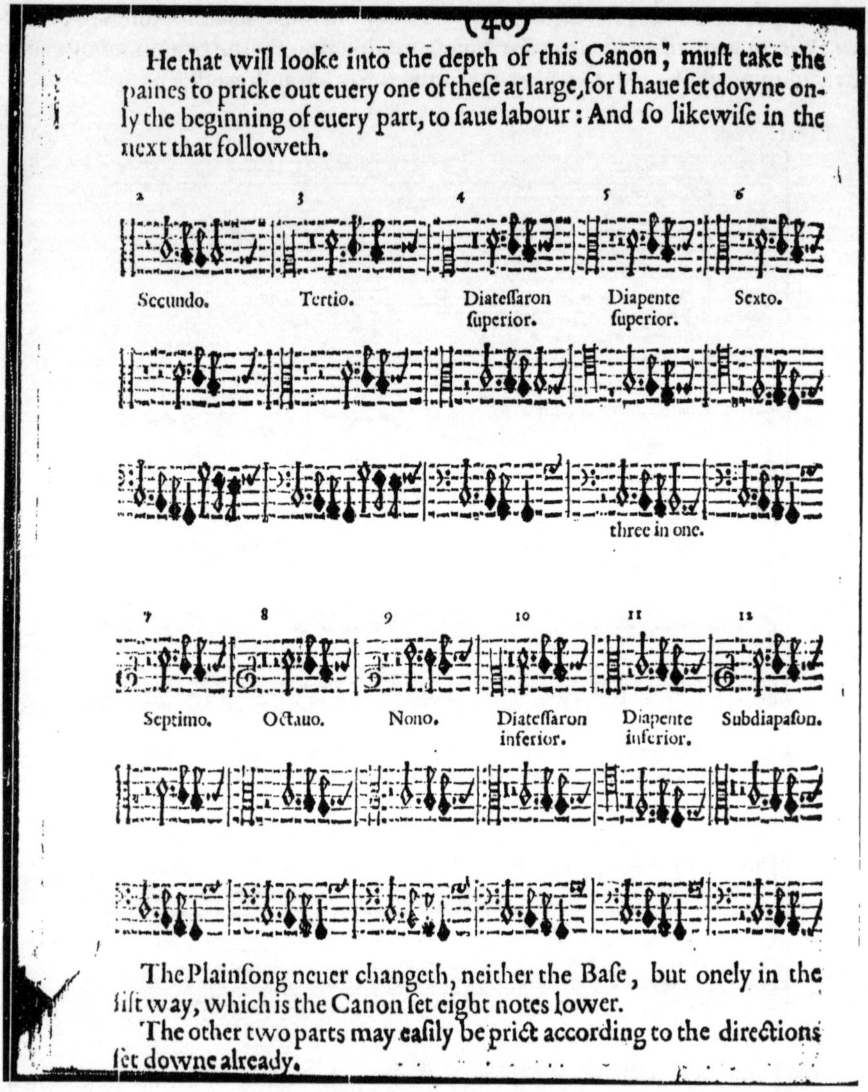

(48)

He that will looke into the depth of this Canon, muſt take the paines to pricke out euery one of theſe at large, for I haue ſet downe only the beginning of euery part, to ſaue labour : And ſo likewiſe in the next that followeth.

Secundo.   Tertio.   Diateſſaron   Diapente   Sexto.
                          ſuperior.   ſuperior.

three in one.

Septimo.   Octauo.   Nono.   Diateſſaron   Diapente   Subdiapaſon.
                                  inferior.   inferior.

The Plainſong neuer changeth, neither the Baſe, but onely in the ſiſt way, which is the Canon ſet eight notes lower.

The other two parts may eaſily be prickt according to the directions ſet downe already.

Figure 4   Page 48, *A Briefe and Short Instruction of the Art of Musicke.* British Library K2.d.14. Used by permission of the British Library and ProQuest Information and Learning Company. Further reproduction is prohibited without permission.

[49] Three parts to the Plain-song, composed in such sort, as euery part is made the Base or ground to the other, which causeth variety of musicke, by reason of the changing of the parts and is to be sung foure seuerall wayes, as appeareth.[ae]

Foure Voc:

[ae]   The second last note in the bass part is corrected from E to G in all copies except British Library K2.d.14, Cambridge and Royal College of Music.

[50] Either of these Replies are to be prict out at large.^{af}

1 The Treble in the first Reply, is the Tenor of the principall, prict an eight higher.
2 The Treble in the second Reply, is the Meane of the principall, prict a fift higher.
3 The Treble in the third Reply, is the Base of the principall, set twelue notes higher.

1 The Meane in the first Reply, is the Treble of the principall.
2 The Meane in the second Reply, is the Base of the principall, set twelue notes higher.
3 The Meane in the third Reply, is the Tenor of the principall, set eight notes higher

1 The Tenor in the first Reply, is the Base of the principall, set eight notes higher.
2 The Tenor in the second Reply, is the Treble of the principall, set eight notes lower.
3 The Tenor in the third Reply, is the Meane of the principall, set foure notes lower.

1 The Base in the first Reply, is the Meane of the principall, set eight notes lower.
2 The Base in the second Reply, is the Tenor of the principall.
3 The Base in the third Reply, is the Treble, set fifteene notes lower.

---

^{af} In the original the written instructions for each part are placed under its corresponding staff in the example.

[51] xxi parts.[20]
Foure parts to the plain-song, euery part fiue in one, resting fiue Semibriefes
after other.[ag]

<hr />

[ag] In the second last bar, a quaver A in the second part from the top is corrected to
C in all copies except British Library K2.d.14, Cambridge and Royal College of Music.

Who so will take a view of all the parts of this song, must take the paine to pricke out euery part by it selfe. The first resteth fiue Semibriefes, the second tenne, the third fifteene, the fourth and last twenty: and so likewise euery Canon.

The Closes that are set here, serue to shew where euery part endeth: The part that resteth fiue Semibriefes, endeth on the last Close saue one, that part that resteth tenne Semibriefes, endeth on the last Close, saue two. So the rest accordingly.

[52] Fiue parts in one to the plain-song, resting fiue Semibriefes after other, in a Round. Thrice ouer.[21]

Sixe Voc.[ah]

<hr>

[ah] A horizontal line that functions as a tie joins the stems of the two notes G in bar 4 of the top part in the Huntington, Library of Congress, British Library RM 15.f.2 and Bodleian copies. These copies and the Royal Academy of Music copy alter 'spiritui' to 'spiritu' in both parts but they do not alter the notes in the leading part to reflect the modified text at this point.

[solution:]

Glo - ri - a ti - bi Do - mi - ne, qui na - tus
Glo - ri - a ti - bi Do - mi - ne, qui na - tus es de Vir - gi - ne
Glo - ri - a ti - bi Do -
es de Vir - gi - ne, cum
cum Pa - - -
- mi - ne, qui na - tus es de Vir - gi - ne
Glo - ri - a ti - bi Do - mi - ne,
Pa - tre et Spi - ri - tu - i san -
-tre et Spi-ri - tu - i san - cto in
cum Pa - - - tre
qui na - tus es de Vir - gi - ne
Glo - ri - a ti - bi Do - mi - ne, qui

Fifteene parts in one, loe here may you see,
Vpon the Plain-song, all contain'd in three.
And to this intent, In fiue notes consist,
That may represent the fiue wounds of Christ.

Canon three in one *per Arsin & Thesin, aliud in Diapason.*[22]

Fiue voc.[ai]

[ai] Fermatas are added over the three final notes in the top part in the Library of Congress, Bodleian, British Library RM 15.f.2 and Huntington copies. The first custos is added in the top part in the Huntington, Library of Congress and British Library RM 15.f.2 copies.

[solution:]

Laus Deo.

Thus much haue I thought sufficient for young Practitioners at this present, but if I may perceiue any to take profit herein, I shall be encouraged hereafter to set out a larger Volume, if it please God to give me life, and enable me thereunto. In the meane season, I wish thee all happinesse and good successe in thy proceedings. Thy harty wel-willer in Christ Iesus, Elway Beuin.

FINIS.

Notes

1   The association of three-part canons and the Trinity is often found in Renaissance music, as evidenced by the numerous Latin canonic inscriptions such as 'Trinitas in Unitas'. This is included in the inscriptions listed by Hermann Finck in his *Musica practica* (Wittenberg: Georg Rhaw, 1556; repr. Bologna: Forni, 1969), sigs. Bb4v–Cc3r. See Bonnie J. Blackburn, 'Two Treasure Chests of Canonic Antiquities: The Collections of Hermann Finck and Lodovico Zacconi', in Katelijne Schiltz and Bonnie J. Blackburn (eds), *Canons and Canonic Techniques, 14th–16th Centuries: Theory, Practice, and Reception History. Proceedings of the International Conference, Leuven, 4–6 October 2005*, Analysis in Context. Leuven Studies in Musicology, 1 (Leuven and Dudley, Mass.: Peeters, 2007), 303–36 at 310 and 328.

2   This piece includes a tonal answer.

3   The numbering '1 Canon' means that this is the first example of a canon at a crotchet distance ('A Crochet following'). The numbering starts over for examples at other distances.

4   This is the first example to include a non-canonic fourth part (the lowest part).

5   The sharp before the note C in bar 5 causes an augmented fifth (F–C♯) between the plainsong and upper part.

6   Only one part is given in the original text; the solution is provided in this edition.

7   This example uses invertible counterpoint at the twelfth, which leads to false relations between the canonic parts at bars 3 and 6.

8   False relations involving B♮ and B♭ result between the canonic parts when invertible counterpoint at the twelfth is employed here. In the first or 'principall' version, this problem is avoided because the note B♮ does not occur in the second canonic part.

9   See Figure 3 (p. 88) for the original notation. The reverse ¢ indicates diminution by half. Therefore, the opening two bars of the leading part are imitated in augmentation and contrary motion. With the change of signature to ¢ in the leading part at bar 3, the following voice is required to imitate in diminution and contrary motion from bar 5, where it gets the reverse ¢ clef, to the end. An awkward moment occurs at the end of bar 5 where the canonic voices have B and A simultaneously. The solution is provided in the edition.

10   The following example is the first in which all of the parts are based on the plainsong. The leading part is set in contrary motion to the plainsong, while the following part is a partial retrograde inversion of the plainsong transposed to G and beginning a bar later.

11   The upper voice imitates the plainsong in contrary motion after a semibreve. The lowest part is a partial retrograde inversion of the plainsong similar to the top voice of the previous example except starting down an octave.

12   The notes of the plainsong are derived by taking alternating notes from the leading part (i.e., D, D, E, D, C, B, A) and transposing them down a fifth in semibreves only.

13   The third canonic part (second from the top), following in double augmentation, treats the dotted crotchet G and quaver A in bar 2 of the leading part as if they were both crotchets.

14   The term 'binding' recalls the examples of 'driuing an odde' crotchet or minim from page 4 of the treatise.

15   In this example the parts are not laid out in score according to range, a feature recalling the manuscript collections attributed to Bevin and Bull. This example also involves contrary motion (*per Arsin & Thesin*).

16   The dotted minim G in the leading part is included among the notes taken by the third part (i.e., the plainsong) and transposed down a fifth.

¹⁷   These instructions indicate that the notes of the plainsong are derived from the leading part in contrary motion and in semibreves only.

¹⁸   Square brackets above notes indicate red-coloured notes and rests in the original text. Also, the opening notes are based on the first plainsong used in the treatise. The solution given by Bevin includes a free bass part.

¹⁹   'This canon comprises twice two and true canons. Two are complete and two are half. Of the latter, each canon requires fifteen [parts]. And firstly, all the other things need to be sung. But a twofold bass is placed beneath; and here you may sing them [*i.e.*, the four canons and the non-canonic parts] singly with nine voices.'

²⁰   The unusual bar length of five semibreves per bar reflects the time distance of the canonic entries. Awkward moments occur with the poorly concealed parallel octaves in bar 5 and the modification of the plainsong in bar 3.

²¹   Five semibreves per bar again reflects the time distance between the parts. This is not maintained in the solution provided in the edition. The presa sign over the first note of the plainsong is redundant.

²²   The solution to this canon, provided in the edition, involves a duplex canon at the octave below based on the ostinato motif, an ornamented version of the plainsong in the tenor, and a free bass part.

Bibliography

Manuscripts

British Library Add. 29996
British Library Add. 30933
British Library Add. 31391
British Library Add. 31403
British Library RM 24.c.14
British Library RM 24.d.7
British Library RM 24.d.12
British Library RM 24.f.25
Cambridge University Library Dd.iv.60
Österreichische Nationalbibliothek Mus. Hs. 17.771

Printed Works

Anonymous, *The Art of Music Collecit out of All Ancient Doctouris of Music*, ed. in Judson Dana Maynard, 'An Anonymous Scottish Treatise on Music from the Sixteenth Century, British Museum, Additional Manuscript 4911, Edition and Commentary' (PhD diss., Indiana University, 1961).

Antoniotto, Giorgio, *L'arte armonica; or a Treatise on the Composition of Music* (London: J. Johnson, 1760).

Bathe, William, *A Briefe Introduction to the Skill of Song*, ed. Kevin C. Karnes (Aldershot: Ashgate, 2005).

Berardi, Angelo, *Documenti armonici* (Bologna: G. Monti, 1687; repr. Bologna: Forni, 1970).

Bevin, Elway, *A Briefe and Short Instruction of the Art of Musicke* (London: R. Young, 1631).

Blackburn, Bonnie J., 'Two Treasure Chests of Canonic Antiquities: The Collections of Hermann Finck and Lodovico Zacconi', in *Canons and Canonic Techniques, 14th–16th Centuries: Theory, Practice, and Reception History. Proceedings of the International Conference, Leuven, 4–6 October 2005*, ed. Katelijne Schiltz and Bonnie J. Blackburn, Analysis in Context. Leuven Studies in Musicology, 1 (Leuven and Dudley, MA: Peeters, 2007), 303–36.

Boetticher, Wolfgang, *Orlando di Lasso und seine Zeit* (Kassel: Bärenreiter, 1958; expanded reissue, Wilhelmshaven: Florian Noetzel, 1999).

Bowling, Lewis P., 'A Transcription and Comparative Analysis of Divers and Sundry Waies of Two Parts in One (1591) by John Farmer' (DA diss., University of Northern Colorado, 1982).

Brett, Philip, 'Did Byrd Write "Non nobis, Domine"?', *Musical Times*, 113/1555 (1972), 855–7.

British Library RM 24.d.2, introduction by Jessie Ann Owens, Renaissance Music in Facsimile, 8 (New York, 1987).

Burn, David, 'Further Observations on Stacked Canon and Renaissance Compositional Procedure: Gascongne's *Ista est speciosa* and Forestier's *Missa L'homme armé*', *Journal of Music Theory*, 45 (2001), 73–118.

Burney, Charles, *A General History of Music from the Earliest Ages to the Present Period*, ed. Frank Mercer, 2 vols. (London: G.T. Foulis, 1935).

Butler, Charles, *The Principles of Musik* (London: John Haviland, 1636).

The Byrd Edition, 17 vols (London: Stainer and Bell, 1976–) (replacing *The Collected Works of William Byrd*, 20 vols, ed. E.H. Fellowes, London, 1937–50; rev. R.T. Dart, 1962–70).

1 *Cantiones Sacrae* (1575), ed. Craig Monson (1977).

16 *Madrigals, Songs and Canons*, ed. Philip Brett (1976).

Caldwell, John, 'Keyboard Plainsong Settings in England, 1500–1660', *Musica Disciplina*, 19 (1965), 129–53.

Calvisius, Seth, *Melopoeia sive melodiae condendae ratio, quam vulgo musicam poeticam vocant* (Erfurt, 1592).

Collins, Denis, 'Bach's Occasional Canon *BWV* 1073 and Stacked Canonic Procedure in the Eighteenth Century', *BACH*, 33/2 (2002), 15–34.

—— 'Canon in Music Theory from c. 1550 to c. 1800' (PhD diss., Stanford University, 1992).

—— '"Sufficient to quench the thirst of the most insaciate scholler whatoever": George Waterhouse's 1,163 Canons on the Plainsong Miserere', in *Canons and Canonic Techniques, 14th–16th Centuries: Theory, Practice, and Reception History. Proceedings of the International Conference, Leuven, 4–6 October 2005*, ed. Katelijne Schiltz and Bonnie J. Blackburn, Analysis in Context. Leuven Studies in Musicology, 1 (Leuven and Dudley, Mass.: Peeters, 2007), 407–20.

—— 'Zarlino and Berardi as Teachers of Canon', *Theoria*, 7 (1993), 103–23.

Cooper, Barry, 'Englische Musiktheorie im 17. und 18. Jahrhundert', in *Entstehung nationaler Traditionen: Frankreich-England. Geschichte der Musiktheorie*, 9 (Darmstadt: Wissenschaftliche Buchgesellschaft, 1986), 141–314.

Danner, Peter K., 'The Miserere Mihi and the English Reformation: A Study of the Evolution of a Cantus Firmus Genre in Tudor Music' (PhD diss., Stanford University, 1967).

Dart, Thurston, 'Purcell and Bull', *Musical Times*, 104/1439 (1963), 30–31.

Del Buono, Giovanni P., *Canoni, oblighi et sonate in varie maniere sopra l'Ave Maris stella* (Palermo: Martarello & d'Angelo, 1641).

Farmer, John, *Divers & Sundry Waies of Two Parts in One, to the Number of Fortie uppon one Playnsong* (London: Thomas East, 1591).

Fellowes, Edmund H., *William Byrd*, 2nd edn (London: Oxford University Press, 1948).

Ferand, Ernest T., 'Improvised Vocal Counterpoint in the Late Renaissance and Early Baroque', *Annales Musicologiques*, 4 (1956), 129–74.

Finck, Hermann, *Musica practica* (Wittenberg: Georg Rhaw, 1556; repr. Bologna: Forni, 1969).

Flynn, Jane, 'The Education of Choristers in England during the Sixteenth Century', in *English Choral Practice 1400–1650*, ed. John Morehen (Cambridge: Cambridge University Press, 1995), 180–99.

Ford, Robert, 'Bevins, Father and Son', *Music Review*, 43 (1982), 104–8.

Gosman, Alan, 'Rameau and Zarlino: Polemics in the *Traité de l'harmonie*', *Music Theory Spectrum*, 22 (2000), 44–59.

——'Stacked Canon and Renaissance Compositional Procedure', *Journal of Music Theory*, 41 (1997), 289–318.

Grimshaw, Julian, 'Morley's Rule for First-Species Canon', *Early Music*, 34 (2006), 661–6.

Haar, James, 'Zarlino's Definition of Fugue and Imitation', *Journal of the American Musicological Society*, 24 (1971), 226–54.

Hawkins, John, *A General History of the Science and Practice of Music*, ed. Charles Cudworth, 2 vols (New York: Dover, 1963).

Herissone, Rebecca, *Music Theory in Seventeenth-Century England*, Oxford Monographs on Music (Oxford: Oxford University Press, 2000).

Hooper, Joseph G., 'Bevin, Elway', *Grove Music Online*, ed. L. Macy. <http://www.grovemusic.com>.

—— *The Life and Work of Elway Bevin* (Bristol, 1971).

Jeans, Susi and Morehen, John, 'Waterhouse, George', *Grove Music Online*, ed. L. Macy. <http://www.grovemusic.com>.

Kollmann, Augustus F.C., *An Essay on Practical Musical Composition* (London: the author, 1799), ed. Imogene Horsley (New York: Da Capo Press, 1973).

Krummel, Donald W., *English Music Printing, 1553–1700* (London: The Biographical Society, 1975).

Lamla, Michael, *Kanonkünste im barocken Italien, insbesondere in Rom* (PhD diss., University of Saarbrücken, 2003).

Lasso, Orlando di, *The Complete Motets*, 11, ed. Peter Bergquist (Madison: A-R Editions, 1995).

Lowinsky, Edward, 'Music in Titian's *Bacchanal of the Andrians*: Origins and History of the *Canon per tonos*', in *Music and Culture of the Renaissance and Other Essays*, 2 vols, ed. Bonnie J. Blackburn (Chicago: University of Chicago Press, 1989), i, 289–350.

Lugge, John, *The Complete Keyboard Works*, ed. Susi Jeans and John Steele (London: Novello, 1990).

Lusitano, Vicente, *Introduttione facilissima et novissima di canto fermo, figurato, contraponto semplice, et in concerto* (Rome, 1553).

Marpurg, Friedrich Wilhelm, *Abhandlung von der Fuge* (Berlin: Haude & Spener, 1753–54).

Maynard, Judson Dana, 'An Anonymous Scottish Treatise on Music from the Sixteenth Century, British Museum, Additional Manuscript 4911, Edition and Commentary' (PhD diss., Indiana University, 1961).

Miller, Hugh M., 'Forty Wayes of 2 pts. In One of Tho[mas] Woodson', *Journal of the American Musicological Society*, 8 (1955), 14–21.

—— '"Pretty Wayes: For young Beginners to Looke on"', *Musical Quarterly*, 33 (1947), 543–56.

—— 'Seventeenth-Century English Faburden Compositions for Keyboard', *Musical Quarterly*, 26 (1940), 50–64.

Morley, Thomas, *A Plaine and Easie Introduction to Practicall Musicke* (London: Peter Short, 1597).

—— *A Plain and Easy Introduction to Practical Music*, ed. R. Alec Harman (New York: W.W. Norton, 1952).

Musica Britannica (Royal Musical Association; London: Stainer and Bell, 1951–).

9 *Jacobean Consort Music*, ed. Thurston Dart and William Coates (1955, rev. 1962, 1971).

59 *Thomas Tomkins: Consort Music*, ed. John Irving (1991).

A New Way of Making Fowre Parts in Counterpoint by Thomas Campion and Rules how to Compose by Giovanni Coprario, ed. Christopher R. Wilson (Aldershot: Ashgate, 2003).

Owens, Jessie A., 'Concepts of Pitch in English Music Theory, c. 1560–1640', in *Tonal Structures in Early Music*, ed. Cristle Collins Judd (New York: Garland, 1998), 183–246.

Pepusch, Johann C., *A Treatise on Harmony*, 2nd edn (London: W. Pearson, 1731; repr. Monuments of Music and Music Literature, 2/28. New York: Broude Bros, 1966).

Playford, John, 'A Brief Introduction to the Art of Descant', in *An Introduction to the Skill of Musick*, 10th edn (London: William Godbid for John Playford, 1683).

—— *A Brief Introduction to the Skill of Musick*, 4th edn (London: William Godbid for John Playford, 1664).

—— *An Introduction to the Skill of Musick* (12th edn rev. Henry Purcell, 1694; reprint ed. Franklin B. Zimmermann, New York: Da Capo Press, 1972).

Purcell, Henry, *Fantazias and Miscellaneous Instrumental Music*, ed. Thurston Dart, rev. Michael Tilmouth, Alan Brown and Peter Holman, The Works of Henry Purcell, 31 (The Purcell Society, London: Novello, 1990).

Ruff, Lillian M., 'The Seventeenth-Century English Music Theorists' (PhD diss., University of Nottingham, 1962).

Schubert, Peter, *Modal Counterpoint, Renaissance Style* (New York: Oxford University Press, 1999).

Simpson, Christopher, *A Compendium of Practical Musick*, 3rd edn (London: H. Brome, 1678 [1st edn 1665; 2nd edn 1667]).

Soden, Geoffrey Ingle, *Godfrey Goodman: Bishop of Gloucester, 1583–1656* (London: S.P.C.K., 1953).

Soriano, Francesco, *Canoni et oblighi di cento et dieci sorte sopra l'Ave maris stella* (Rome: G.B. Robletti, 1610).

Spink, Ian, 'Child, William', *Grove Music Online*, ed. L. Macy. <http://www.grovemusic.com>.

Strahle, Graham, *An Early Music Dictionary: Musical Terms from British Sources, 1500–1740* (Cambridge: Cambridge University Press, 1995).

Sweelinck, Jan Pieterszoon, *Werken*, 10, ed. H. Gehrmann (Leipzig: Breitkopf & Härtel, 1901).

Tansur, William, *The Elements of Musick Display'd* (London: Stanley Crowder, 1772).

Tigrini, Oratio, *Il compendiolo della musica* (Venice: Ricciardo Amadino, 1558; facs. edn New York: Broude Bros., 1966).

Tomkins, Thomas, *Consort Music*, ed. John Irving, Musica Britannica, 59 (London: Stainer and Bell, 1991).

Van der Meer, John H., 'The Keyboard Works in the Vienna Bull Manuscript', *Tijdschrift voor Muziekwetenschap*, 43 (1959), 72–105.

Vicentino, Nicola, *L'antica musica ridotta alla moderna prattica* (Rome: Antonio Barre, 1555; facs. ed. Edward Lowinsky, Kassel: Bärenreiter, 1959).

Walker, Paul, 'The Origin of the Permutation Fugue', in *The Creative Process. Studies in the History of Music*, 3 (New York: Broude Bros. Ltd., 1992), 51–91.

Zarlino, Gioseffo, *Le istitutioni harmoniche* (Venice: F. Senese, 1558, rev. 1573). Pt. 3 (1558) trans. as *The Art of Counterpoint*, by Guy Marco and Claude Palisca (New Haven: Yale University Press, 1968).

Index

References to music examples and other illustrations are in **bold**.